I0162089

The Poetry of Thomas Parnell

Volume II

The Poet Thomas Parnell was born in Ireland on 11th September 1679. He was the descendant of an ancient family, which had been settled for hundreds of years at Congleton in Cheshire. His father, also named Thomas, took the side of the Commonwealth, and at the Restoration went over to Ireland, where he purchased a considerable property. This, along with his estate in Cheshire, devolved to the poet and was to provide an income of rents with which the young Parnell could embrace life.

At school he is said to have distinguished himself by the retentiveness of his memory; often performing the task allotted for days in a few hours, and being able to repeat forty lines in any book of poems, after the first reading.

He entered Trinity College Dublin at the unusually early age of thirteen and took the degree of M.A. in 1700. The same year (although a dispensation was needed on account of his being under age) he was ordained deacon by the Bishop of Derry. Three years after, he was ordained a priest; and in 1705, he was made Archdeacon of Clogher, by Sir George Ashe, bishop of that see.

On receipt of the archdeanery, he married Miss Ann Minchin, described as a young lady of great beauty, and of an amiable character, by whom he had two sons, who tragically, died young, and a daughter, who was to survive both parents.

Up to the fall of the Whigs, at the end of Queen Anne's reign, Parnell appears to have been, like his father, a keen supporter. He now switched political allegiance to the Tories and was hailed as a valuable addition to their ranks.

Parnell was blessed with great social qualities and soon fell in with the brilliant set of literary figures; Pope, Swift, Gay. He became a member of the Scriblerus Club , an informal gathering of authors, based in London, in the early 18th century. Prominent figures from the Augustan Age of English letters were members; Jonathan Swift, Alexander Pope, John Gay, John Arbuthnot and Henry St. John. Founded in 1714 the club lasted until the death of the founders, finally ending in 1745. At about his time Parnell also wrote in the "Spectator."

To Pope, he was of essential service, assisting him in his notes to the "Iliad," being, what Pope was not, a good Greek scholar. He wrote a life of Homer, which was prefixed to the Translation, although stiff in style, and flamboyant in statement.

Parnell first visited London in 1706; and from that period till his death, scarcely a year elapsed without his spending some time in the great metropolis.

As soon as he had collected his rents, he would travel to London to enjoy himself though he continued to preach and his sermons were popular even if it appears they were more of the 'showman' type.

As each London furlough expired, he returned to Ireland, jaded and dispirited, and there took delight in nursing his melancholy; in pining for the amusements of what he had left behind; shunning and sneering at the society around him; and in abusing his native bogs and his fellow-countrymen in verse.

In 1712 he lost his wife, with whom he appears to have lived as happily as his morbid temperament and mortified feelings would permit. This blow deepened his melancholy, and drove him, it is said, to excessive drinking.

Later that same year and back in London, and once more under the "special patronage" of Dean Swift, and who wished, through his side, to mortify certain persons in Ireland, who did not appreciate, he says, the Archdeacon; and who, we suspect, besides, did not thoroughly appreciate the Dean. Swift, partly in pity for the "poor lad," as he calls him, whom he saw to be in such imminent danger of losing caste and character, and partly in the true patronising spirit, introduced Parnell to Lord Bolingbroke, who received him kindly, entertained him at dinner, and encouraged him in his poetical studies but did little else. The consequences of dissipation began, at this time, too, to appear in Parnell's constitution; and we find Swift saying of him, "His head is out of order, like mine, but more constant, poor boy." It was perhaps to this period that Pope referred, when he told Spence, "Parnell is a great follower of drams, and strangely open and scandalous in his debaucheries." If so, his bad habits seem to have sprung as much from disappointment and discontent as from taste.

Yet Swift continued to help his friend, and it was at his instance that, in 1713, Archbishop King presented Parnell with a prebend (a portion of the revenues of a cathedral or collegiate church formerly granted to a canon or member of the chapter as his stipend).

In 1714, his hope of London promotion died with Queen Anne; but in 1716, the same generous Archbishop bestowed on him the vicarage of Finglass, in the diocese of Dublin, worth £400 a-year.

However Thomas Parnell did not live long enough to enjoy the full benefit. He died at Chester, about to leave for Ireland, on 24 October 1718.

As a poet his legacy was not of the first order but his poems were greatly appreciated as were his skills as essayist and translator and obviously as a clergyman his talents seemed to have ensured promotion but quite how observant he was given his excess is difficult to judge.

Parnell's poetry is lyrical and often is written in heroic couplets. It was said of his poetry 'it was in keeping with his character, easy and pleasing, enunciating the common places with felicity and grace.' He was also one of the so-called "Graveyard poets": his 'A Night-Piece on Death,' widely considered the first "Graveyard School" poem, which was published posthumously in Poems on Several Occasions, collected and edited by his great friend Alexander Pope.

Index of Poems

Thou Gaudy Idle world adieu,
& all thy tinsell Joys;
I lovd thee dearly once tis true,
But since a better choice I knew,
Ive made that better choice.
My wishes mount above the sky
Upon the wings of faith,
My soul shall follow when I dy,
For much I doubt if bodys fly,
What ever Asgill saith.
All things are fickle here below,
How ere above they be,
& If I had not left thee now,
Thy pleasures had left me.
Count but the changes Memory
Which your short time has known,
This is the third King which you see
Upon the English throne.
The Irish who by Williams reign
Were run so much aground,
Do by the Trust (confound it) Gain
three hundred thousand pound.
& My acquaintance wonder not
When you my change discover
Ev'n Methwin has a prayr book bought
'Gainst Rochester comes over.

The Flies — An Ecologue

When in the River Cows for Coolness stand,
And Sheep for Breezes seek the lofty Land,
A Youth whom Æsop taught that ev'ry Tree
Each Bird and Insect spoke as well as he:
Walk'd calmly musing in a shaded Way
Where flow'ring Hawthorn broke the sunny Ray,
And thus instructs his Moral Pen to draw
A Scene that obvious in the Field he saw.

Near a low Ditch, where shallow Waters meet,
Which never learnt to glide with liquid Feet,
Whose Naiads never prattle as they play,
But screen'd with Hedges slumber out the Day,
There stands a slender Fern's aspiring Shade,
Whose answ'ring Branches regularly layd
Put forth their answ'ring Boughs, and proudly rise
Three Stories upward, in the nether Skies.

For Shelter here, to shun the Noon-day Heat,

An airy Nation of the Flies retreat;
Some in soft Air their silken Pinions ply,
And some from Bough to Bough delighted fly,
Some rise, and circling light to perch again;
A pleasing Murmur hums along the Plain.
So, when a Stage invites to pageant Shows,
(If great and small are like) appear the Beaus,
In Boxes some with spruce Pretension sit,
Some change from Seat to Seat within the Pit,
Some roam the Scenes, or turning cease to roam;
Preluding Musick fills the lofty Dome.

When thus a Fly (if what a Fly can say
Deserves attention) rais'd the rural Lay.

Where late Amintor made a Nymph a Bride,
Joyful I flew by young Favonia's side,
Who, mindless of the Feasting, went to sip
The balmy Pleasure of the Shepherd's Lip.
I saw the Wanton, where I stoop'd to sup,
And half resolv'd to drown me in the Cup;
'Till brush'd by careless Hands, she soar'd above:
Cease, Beauty, cease to vex a tender Love.

Thus ends the Youth, the buzzing Meadow rung,
And thus the Rival of his Musick sung.

When Suns by thousands shone in Orbs of Dew,
I wafted soft with Zephyretta flew;
Saw the clean Pail, and sought the milky Chear,
While little Daphne seiz'd my roving Dear.
Wretch that I was! I might have warn'd the Dame,
Yet sat indulging as the Danger came,
But the kind Huntress left her free to soar:
Ah! guard, ye Lovers, guard a Mistress more.

Thus from the Fern, whose high-projecting Arms,
The fleeting Nation bent with dusky Swarms,
The Swains their Love in easy Musick breathe,
When Tongues and Tumult stun the Field beneath.
Black Ants in Teams come darkning all the Road,
Some call to march, and some to lift the Load;
They strain, they labour with incessant Pains
Press'd by the cumbrous weight of single Grains.
The Flies struck silent gaze with Wonder down:
The busy Burghers reach their earthy Town;
Where lay the Burthens of a wint'ry Store,
And thence unwearied part in search of more.
Yet one grave Sage a Moment's space attends,
And the small City's loftiest Point ascends,
Wipes the salt Dew that trickles down his Face,

And thus harangues them with the gravest Grace.

Ye foolish Nurslings of the Summer Air,
These gentle Tunes and whining Songs forbear;
Your Trees and whisp'ring Breeze, your Grove and Love,
Your Cupids Quiver, and his Mother's Dove:
Let Bards to Business bend their vig'rous Wing,
And sing but seldom, if they love to sing:
Else, when the Flourets of the Season fail,
And this your Ferny Shade forsakes the Vale,
Tho' one would save ye, not one Grain of Wheat
Shou'd pay such Songsters idling at my Gate.

He ceas'd: The Flies, incorrigibly vain,
Heard the May'r's Speech, and fell to sing again.

On Queen Anne's Peace, Anno 1713

Mother of plenty, daughter of the skies,
Sweet Peace, the troubl'd world's desire, arise;
Around thy poet weave thy summer shades,
Within my fancy spread thy flow'ry meads,
Amongst thy train soft ease and pleasure bring,
And thus indulgent sooth me whilst I sing.

Great Anna claims the song; no brighter name
Adorns the list of never-dying fame,
No fairer soul was ever form'd above,
None e'er was more the grateful nation's love
Nor lov'd the nation more. I fly with speed
To sing such lines as Bolingbroke may read,
On war dispers'd, on faction trampled down,
On all the peaceful glories of the crown.
And if I fail in too confin'd a flight,
May the kind world upon my labours write;
'So fell the lines which strove for endless fame,
'Yet fell attempting on the noblest theme.

Now twelve revolving years has Britain stood
With loss of wealth and vast expence of blood
Europa's Guardian; still her gallant arms
Secur'd Europa from impending harms.
Fair honour, full success, and just applause,
Pursu'd her marches, and adorn'd her cause;
Whilst Gaul, aspiring to erect a throne
O'er other empires, trembled for her own,
Bemoan'd her cities won, her armies slain,
And sunk the thought of universal reign.

When thus reduc'd the world's Invaders lie,
The fears which rack'd the nations, justly die:
Pow'r finds its balance, giddy motions cease
In both the scales, and each inclines to peace.
This fair occasion Providence prepares,
To answer pious Anna's hourly pray'rs,
Which still on warm Devotion's wings arose,
And reaching Heav'n obtain'd the world's repose.

Within the vast expansion of the sky,
Where Orbs of gold in fields of Azure lie,
A glorious palace shines, whose silver ray
Serenely flowing lights the milky way,
The road of angels. Here with speedy care
The summon'd Guardians of the world repair.
When Britain's Angel on the message sent
Speaks Anna's pray'rs and Heaven's supream intent,
That war's destructive arm shou'd humble Gaul,
Spain's parted realms to diff'rent monarchs fall,
The grand alliance crown'd with glory cease,
And joyful Europe find the sweets of peace.
He spoke: the smiling hopes of man's repose,
The joy that springs from certain hopes arose
Diffusive o'er the place; complacent airs
Sedately sweet were heard within the spheres;
And bowing all adore the sovereign mind,
And fly to execute the work design'd.

This done, the Guardian on the wing repairs
Where Anna sat revolving publick cares
With deep concern of thought. Unseen he stood
Presenting peaceful images of good
On Fancy's airy stage; returning Trade,
A sunk Exchequer fill'd, an Army paid,
The fields with men, the men with plenty bless'd,
The towns with riches, and the world with rest.
Such pleasing objects on her bosom play,
And give the dawn of glory's golden day,
When all her labours at their harvest shewn
Shall in her subjects joy compleat her own.
Then breaking silence, 'tis enough, she cries,
That war has rag'd to make the nations wise.
Heav'n prospers armies whilst they fight to save,
And thirst of further fame destroys the brave;
The vanquish'd Gauls are humbly pleas'd to live,
And but escap'd the chains they meant to give.
Now let the pow'rs be still'd and each possess'd
Of what secures the common safety best.

So spake the Queen, then fill'd with warmth divine
She call'd her Oxford to the grand design;

Her Oxford prudent in affairs of state,
Profoundly thoughtful, manifestly great
In ev'ry turn, whose steddy temper steers
Above the reach of gold or shock of fears;
Whom no blind chance, but merit understood
By frequent tryals, pow'r of doing good,
And will to execute, advanc'd on high,
O soul created to deserve the sky!
And make the nation, crown'd with glory, see
How much it rais'd itself by raising thee!
Now let the schemes which labour in thy breast
The long Alliance bless with lasting rest:
Weigh all pretences with impartial laws,
And fix the sep'rate Int'rests of the cause.

These toils the graceful Bolingbroke attends,
A Genius fashion'd for the greatest ends,
Whose strong perception takes the swiftest flight,
And yet its swiftness ne'er obscures its sight:
When schemes are fix'd, and each assign'd a part,
None serves his country with a nobler heart,
Just thoughts of honour all his mind controul,
And Expedition wings his lively soul.
On such a Patriot to confer the Trust,
The Monarch knows it safe as well as just.

Then next proceeding in her Agents choice
And ever pleas'd that worth obtain the voice,
She from the list of high-distinguish'd fames
With pious Bristow gallant Strafford names:
One form'd to stand a church's firm support,
The other fitted to adorn a court,
Both vers'd in business, both of fine address,
By which experience leads to great success:
And both to distant lands the Monarch sends,
And to their conduct Europe's peace commends.

Now ships unmoor'd to waft her Agents o'er
Spread all their sail, and quit the flying shore.
The foreign Agents reach th' appointed place,
The Congress opens, and it will be peace.
Methinks the war like stormy winter flies,
When fairer months unveil the blueish skies,
A flow'ry world the sweetest season spreads,
And doves with branches flutter round their heads.

Half-peopled Gaul whom num'rous ills destroy
With wishful heart attends the promis'd joy.
For this prepares the Duke—ah sadly slain
'Tis grief to name him whom we mourn in vain:
No warmth of verse repairs the vital flame,

For verse can only grant a life in fame,
Yet cou'd my praise like spicy odours shed
In everlasting song embalm the dead,
To realms that weeping heard the loss I'd tell,
What courage, sense, and faith, with Brandon fell.

But Britain more than one for glory breeds,
And polish'd Talbot to the charge succeeds,
Whose far-projecting thoughts maturely clear
Like glasses draw their distant objects near.
Good Parts by gentle breeding much refin'd,
And stores of learning grace his ample mind,
A cautious virtue regulates his ways,
And Honour gilds them with a thousand rays.
To serve his nation at his Queen's command,
He parts commission'd for the Gallick land:
With pleasure Gaul beholds him on her shore
And learns to love a name she fear'd before.

Once more aloft there meet for new debates
The Guardian Angels of Europa's states:
And mutual concord shines in ev'ry face
And ev'ry bosom glows with hopes of peace,
While Britain's steps in one consent they praise,
Then gravely mourn their other realms delays,
Their doubtful claims through seas of blood pursu'd,
Their fears that Gallia fell but half subdu'd,
And all the reas'nings which attempt to shew
That war shou'd ravage in the world below.
'Ah fall'n estate of man! can rage delight!
'Wounds please the touch, or ruin charm the sight!
'Ambition make unlovely mischief fair!
'Or ever Pride be Providence's care!
'When stern Oppressors range the bloody field,
''Tis just to conquer and unsafe to yield:
'There save the nations; but no more pursue
'Nor in thy turn become Oppressor too.'
Our rebel angels for Ambition fell,
And war in Heav'n produc'd a Fiend in hell.
Thus with a soft concern for man's repose
The tender Guardians join to moan our woes,
Then awful rise, combin'd with all their might,
To find what Fury 'scap'd the den of night
The pleasing labours of their love withstands,
And spreads a wild distraction o'er the lands.
Their glitt'ring pinnions sound in yielding air,
And watchful Providence approves the care.

In Flandria's soil where Camps have mark'd the plain,
The Fiend, impetuous Discord, fix'd her reign;
A tent her royal seat. With full resort

Stern shapes of Horrour throng'd her buisy court,
Blind Mischief, Ambush close concealing Ire,
Loud Threat'nings, Ruin arm'd with sword and fire,
Assaulting Fierceness, Anger wanting breath,
High Red'ning Rage, and Various Forms of death,
Dire Imps of darkness, whom with Gore she feeds
When war beyond its point of Good proceeds.
In Gallick armour, call'd with alter'd name
Great love of Empire, to the field she came;
Now, still supporting Feud, she strives to hide
Beneath that name, and only change the side:
But as she whirl'd the rapid wheels around
Where mangl'd limbs in heaps pollute the ground,
(A sullen Joyless Sport,) with searching eye
The shining Chiefs regard her as they fly,
Then hov'ring, dart their beams of heav'nly light,
She starts, the Fury stands confess'd to sight,
And grieves to leave the soil, and yells aloud,
Her Yells are answer'd by the Sable Crowd,
And all on Bat-like wings (if Fame be true)
From Christian lands to Northern climates flew.

But rising murmours from Britannia's shore
With speed recal her watchful Guardian o'er.
He spreads his pinions, and approaching near,
These hints in scatter'd words assault his ear,
The People's Pow'r—The Grand Alliance cross'd
The Peace is sep'rate—Our Religion's lost.
Led by the Blatant voice along the skies,
He comes where Faction over cities flies;
A talking Fiend whom snaky locks disgrace,
And num'rous mouths deform her dusky face,
Whence Lies are utter'd, Whisper softly sounds,
Sly Doubts amaze, or Innuendo wounds.
Within her arms are heaps of Pamphlets seen,
And these blaspheme the Saviour, those the Queen;
Associate Vices: thus with tongue and hand
She shed her venom o'er the troubled land.
Now vex'd that Discord and the Baneful Train
That tends on Discord, fled the neighb'ring plain,
She rag'd to madness: when the Guardian came,
And downwards drove her with a sword of flame.
A mountain gaping to the Nether Hell
Receiv'd the Fury railing as she fell:
The mountain closing o'er the Fury lies,
And stops her passage where she means to rise,
And when she strives, or shifts her side for ease,
All Britain rocks amidst her circling seas.

Now Peace returning after tedious woes
Restores the comforts of a calm repose:

Then bid the Warriors sheath their sanguin'd arms,
Bid Angry Trumpets cease to sound Alarms,
Guns leave to thunder in the tortur'd air,
Red streaming colours furl around the spear,
And each contending realm no longer jarr,
But pleas'd with rest unharness all the war.

She comes the Blessing comes, where'er she moves
New springing Beauty all the land improves:
More heaps of fragrant flow'rs the field adorn,
More sweet the Birds salute the Rosy Morn,
More lively Green refreshes all the leaves,
And in the Breeze the corn more thickly waves.
She comes the Blessing comes in easy state,
And Forms of Brightness all around her wait:
Here smiling Safety with her bosom bare
Securely walks, and chearful Plenty there;
Here wond'rous Sciences with Eagles sight,
There Liberal Arts which make the world polite,
And open Traffick joining hand in hand
With honest Industry, approach the land.

O welcome long desir'd and lately found!
Here fix thy seat upon the British ground,
Thy Shining Train around the Nation send,
While by degrees the loading Taxes end:
While Caution, calm yet still prepar'd for arms,
And Foreign Treaties, guard from foreign harms:
While equal Justice hearing ev'ry cause
Makes ev'ry Subject join to love the laws.

Where Britain's Patriots in Council meet
Let publick safety rest at Anna's feet:
Let Oxford's schemes the Path to Plenty shew
And through the realm increasing Plenty go.
Let Arts and Sciences in glory rise,
And pleas'd the world has leisure to be wise,
Around their Oxford and their St. John stand,
Like Plants that flourish by the Master's hand:
And safe in hope the sons of Learning wait
Where Learning's Self has fix'd her fair retreat.
Let Traffick cherish'd by the Senate's care
On all the seas employ the wafting air:
And Industry with circulating wing
Through all the land the goods of Traffick bring.
The Blessings so dispos'd will long abide,
Since Anna reigns, and Harley's thoughts preside;
Great Ormond's arms the sword of Caution wield,
And hold Britannia's broad-protecting Shield;
Bright Bolingbroke and worthy Dartmouth treat
By fair dispatch with ev'ry foreign State;

And Harcourt's knowledge equitably shewn
Makes Justice call his firm Decrees her own.

Thus all that Poets fanci'd Heav'n of old
May for the nation's present Emblem hold:
There Jove imperial sway'd; Minerva wise,
And Phœbus eloquent, adorn'd the skies;
On Arts Cyllenius fix'd his full delight,
Mars rein'd the War, and Themis judg'd the Right:
All mortals once beneficently great,
(As Fame reports) and rais'd in Heav'nly State;
Yet sharing labours, still they shun'd repose,
To shed the blessings down by which they rose.

Illustrious Queen, how Heav'n hath heard thy pray'rs,
What stores of Happiness attend thy Cares!
A Church in safety fix'd, a State in rest,
A Faithful Ministry, a People bless'd,
And Kings submissive at thy foot-stool thrown,
That others Rights restore, or beg their own.
Now rais'd with thankful mind, and rolling slow,
In grand Procession to the temple go,
By snow-white Horses drawn; while sounding Fame
Proclaims thy coming, Praise exalts thy name,
Fair Honour dress'd in robes adorns thy state,
And on thy Train the crowded Nations wait,
Who pressing view with what a temper'd grace
The looks of Majesty compose thy face,
And mingling Sweetness shines, or how thy dress
And how thy Pomp an inward Joy confess,
Then fill'd with Pleasures to thy glory due
With Shouts the Chariot moving on pursue.

As when the Phœnix from Arabia flown,
(If any Phœnix were like Anna known,)
His spice at Phœbus Shrine prepar'd to lay,
Where'er their Monarch cut his airy way
The gath'ring Birds around the Wonder flew,
And much admir'd his Shape and much his Hue,
The tuft of Gold that glow'd above his head,
His spacious Train with golden feathers spread,
His gilded Bosom speck'd with purple pride,
And both his Wings in glossy purple dy'd:
He still pursues his way, with wond'ring eyes
The Birds attend, and follow where he flies.

Thrice happy Britons, if at last you know,
'Tis less to conquer than to want a foe;
That Triumphs still are made for War's decrease,
When Men by Conquest rise to views of Peace;
That over Toils for Peace in view we run,

Which gain'd, the World is pleas'd, and War is done.
Fam'd Blenheim's field, Ramillies noble seat,
Blaregni's desperate act of gallant heat,
Or wond'rous Winendale, are war pursu'd
By wounds and deaths through plains with blood embru'd;
But good Design to make the world be still,
With human Grace adorns the needful Ill;
This end obtain'd, we close the Scenes of rage
And gentler Glories deck the rising age.

Such gentler Glories, such reviving days,
The Nation's wishes, and the Statesman's praise,
Now pleas'd to shine in golden Order throng,
Demand our Annals and enrich our Song.
Then go where Albion's Cliffs approach the skies,
(The Fame of Albion so deserves to rise)
And deep engrav'd for Time 'till Time shall cease,
Upon the Stones their fair Inscription place.
Iberia rent, the Pow'r of Gallia broke,
Batavia rescu'd from the threat'ned Yoke,
The royal Austrian rais'd, his Realms restor'd,
Great Britain arm'd, triumphant and ador'd,
Its State enlarg'd, its Peace restor'd again,
Are Blessings all adorning Anna's Reign.

Oh Tell If Any Fate You See

O Tell if any fate you see
Can more unhappy prove
Than where the nymph will cruell be
& still the swain must love
Twere Joy to sigh & serve a fair
Coud sighs & service gain
But if they not availing are
they grow the lovers pain
Damon as thus he spoke his grief
Thought all around him pind
But Celia bringing no relief
He Car'd not what was kind

Martial

For Nothing Lucy never plays ye whore
Thats true—for Lucy ever pays before

On the Trust

Think England what it is to shake,
& better use your King,
His power raisd the frozen snake,
& Must he when he hears it speak,
Find how the tongue can sting?
Trustees you make in long debates,
Which he is forcd to give;
While by your trust the rebell getts,
The subject looses bought estates,
& the oppressors live.
Pitty us heaven, & lend your aid,
Anothers intrest sett us free,
& now it gives us slavery,
Thus weakness is a property,
& Greatness still obeyd.
The men whose heavy arms we feel
By Politicks are good or ill,
Deceiving, or deceivd;
Their law is founded on their will,
& our's by that inslavd.
Against their princes acts they rise,
& in their princes name;
The sly intreaguing factions choice,
& erring patriots shame.
So Dunghill foggs by fiery rays
To saucy empire scale,
Obscure the royall planetts face,
With pride supply a lofty place,
& with out pitty fall.

In Biddy's Cheeks Ye Roses Blow

In Biddy's Cheeks ye roses blow
In Cattys nose they rise
From Biddys lips soft accents flow
And streams from Catty's Eyes
The jet that Biddy's brows display
To Catty's teeth repairs
And Biddy's Lillies bleachd to grey
Appear in Catty's hairs
Yet all ye world sweet Biddy toast
Neglected Catty lyes
While she deserves ye Bumper most
Who most attracts our Eyes

On Mr Collier's Essay On the Stage

Some ages has the stage triumphant stood,
And vice in masquerade debauchd the crowd;
In charming numbers, all bewitching arts,
Has the gay syren drest to steal our hearts:
Like undesigning pleasure she appears,
At once delights & unperceivd insnares,
Long has she found th' unhappy pow'r to please,
& wantond in a luxury of success.
But you unmasque the fashionable cheat,
Draw off the curtain, & dissect the bait,
Expose to view the hook so closely hid,
Break down her altars, & her priests deride.
Thus, when to painted Idols Israel bowd,
The good Elijah Zealous for his god
Against the blocks, and all their prophets rose,
Alone attackd and overthrew his foes.

Hail man of god, all hail, whose pious quill
Dares check a world thats so perversly ill,
Dares ev'n its darling vanities abuse,
And in its full Carreer arrest the looser muse.
You like some angell guide conduct us on,
& shew the sodom wch you teach to shun;
You spoil the varnisht ill of all its rays,
Of all its beauty's, evry borrowd grace,
& shew wt lurks beneath so smooth a face.

Thus (say the bards) some worthy knight maintains
A warr wth fairy states, enchanted scenes,
When he moves on the bright delusion fly's,
& dismall dungeons gape before his eyes

On Happiness in This Life

The morning opens very freshly gay
And life itself is in the month of May.
With green my fancy paints an arbour o'er
And flowrets with a thousand colours more;
Then falls to weaving that, and spreading these
And softly shakes them with an easy breeze,
With golden fruit adorns the bending shade,
Or trails a silver water o'er its bed.
Glide, gentle water, still more gently by
While in this summer-bower of bliss I lye
And sweetly sing of sense delighting flames,
And nymphs and shepherds soft invented names,
Or view the branches which around me twine

And praise their fruit, diffusing sprightly wine,
Or find new pleasures in the world to praise
And still with this return adorn my lays;
'Range round your gardens of eternal spring,
'Go range my senses while I sweetly sing.'

In vain, in vain alas, seduc'd by ill
And acted wildly by the force of will!
I tell my soul it will be constant May,
And Charm a season never made to stay,
My beauteous arbour will not stand a storm,
The world but promises, and can't perform:
Then fade ye leaves and wither all ye flow'rs,
I'll doat no longer in enchanted bow'rs;
But sadly mourn in melancholy song,
The vain conceits that held my soul so long.
The lusts that tempt us with delusive show,
And sin brought forth for everlasting woe.
Thus shall the notes to sorrow's object rise,
While frequent rests procure a place for sighs;
And as I moan upon the naked plain,
Be this the burthen closing ev'ry strain;
Return my senses, range no more abroad,
He'll only find his bliss, who seeks for God.

On Ye Bishop of Meaths Death

Mourn widdowd lland, Mourn, your Pan is dead.
Mourn ye unhappy flocks your Sheapherd Pan is fled;
Around your grief in dolefull straines convey,
& Lett ym in sad Eccho's dy away,
As sympathising wth their masters care,
As if they felt th' unlucky newes they bear,
Of this so true a saint heav'n seem'd to send him here.
To shew how good in innocence we were:
So true a saint.
We thought he was no man, but from ye skyes
(as there were oft of old) some angell in disguise,
But see to undeceive us to our grief, he dies.
He was with so good thoughts so freely springing blest,
ye divine garden so few briars did molest,
As if a Paradise were in his breast.
Serene his mind as heaven did appear;
His lookes serene as mercy's self might wear;
His actions might in Justice scales be try'd;
When ere he speak & heav'n a theam suppli'd,
Hed melt ye rockiest hearts like Moses to a tide.
But now he setts, his paines & toiles are o're,
& heav'n rewards ye seer with all his store:

He's spent wth doing good, & now lies down at ease
Stretcht on ye Pillows of æternall peace.
So ye fam'd Pithian Priestess when her soul
With ye demanded Oracle is full,
Vext with ye God yt rages in her breast,
Nature is tir'd, her spirits are opprest,
She flyes to sacred groves, & sinkes away to rest.

Concerning Resolution

Happy the man whose firm resolves obtain
Assisting Grace to burst his sinfull chain
For him the Days with golden minutes glow
Tis his the Land where milk & hony flow
Justice & mercy piety & peace
Attend his workes & crown them with success
He hopes the best that is for heavn prepard
& wants no bliss while virtue can reward
That purpled hour which ushers in the light
& that which shuts its beautys up in night
Still hears him pray still sees his actions right
For him they still on easy minutes speed
& as they move for him the rest succeed

But most Alas by vain opinion lead
Ore the wild maze of erring passions tread
& now to this & now to that we go
& each desire & neither rightly know
& act irresolute in all we do
& seldom stay to search our objects through
Desire is vain & wanton free to range
Fond of a Chace & fond the Chace to Change
By turns a thousand inclinations rise
& each by turns as impotently dies
Now thought grows wild if loose Aminta's kind
Shee spreads her Charms & captivates the mind
Anon Aminta leaves the thought at ease
No more her aires & soft Allurements please
We love reclining in ye shady bowers
by running waters near sweet banks of flowrs
To surfeit nature with full bowles of wine
& with forcd appetites on bliss refine
Then buisy then fantastically wise
Then to be some thing else we streight devise
For Fancy still undreind affors supplys
Tis thus if reason from the throne be gon
The madd affections bear their master on
His life proves restless & his labour vain
By hurrying after Phantomes of the brain

So the brave Falcon when its glorys fade
When its strong wings their generous forces shed
The vacant holds ignobler birds supply
With Ravens feathers impd she mounts on high
& weak or giddy strayes along the sky

In Every Change indeed resolves we make
But those resolves to settle newer break
By contradictions thus we seem to live
Nor want the colour of a cause to give
Kind heav'n forgive us when for what we do
We woud debauch our knack of reasning too
When int'rest does on thought its force dispence
When pleasure beats upon the dazzled sence
Our resolutions oft in vain are made
Kind heavn forgive the fault & lend thine aid.
If by thy law we must temptations find
If these must try the temper of the mind
We begg thee not to change thy good decree
We begg for pardon or support from thee
Our wisdome never shoud thy ways confine
but thus confess & humbly rest in thine
Tis well theres tryalls since the mans so proud
& since he's weak tis well theres Grace allowd.

Phillis I Long Yr Powr Have Ownd

Phillis I long yr powr have ownd
& you still gently swayd
Now nature has yr charms dethrond
& time your chain decayd
Both are wth such perversness curst
They still would bliss destroy
This change approves tho' for ye worst
That makes the best things cloy
Try then the forces of disdain
Since kindness wins not me
For know you must to rule again
Another woman be.

A Divine Pastorall

Strephon & I upon a bank were laid,
Where the gay spring in varied colours playd,
& her rich odours lavish nature shed.
When thus the Youth, while this we wondring view
Can we but wonder at its maker too,
Amintas, if I know him, did not use

Shoud such a subject call, to want a muse,
Oh sing the great, the wise creating powr,
While silent I admire, & in your words adore.
Then I, for long before the thought was mine,
Did thus to meet the good demand begin.

Ye Mountains, & ye hills which lower rise,
Ye humble vallies, & ye spreading trees,
Ye pleasant meadows, & thou easy stream,
O praise the Lord, O magnify his name!
Yes, as you can you tell his name abroad,
The wondrous work proclaims the worker God.
Gently awhile sweet Breezes move along,
Then swiftly bear aloft my finisht song.

Ye tame & savage beasts in one accord,
Joyn with all these to Glorify the Lord;
Ye Birds, Ye tunefull birds in him rejoyce,
Give him your musick, who gave you your voice,
Hark how the cheerfull labour of their throats,
Returns the tribute of their pretty notes.
Gently awhile sweet Breezes move along,
Then swiftly bear aloft my rising song.

But still the earth, & still the seas are mute,
The Birds are speechless, speechless is the Brute,
Man that alone can speak his praise must doo't.
Praise him O man with a transported heart,
Let the melodious hand confess its art,
Let the raisd voice his bounteous glory's sing,
Shoud less be joynd to praise so great a King?
Gently awhile sweet Breezes move along,
Then swiftly bear aloft my rising song.

For thee the seasons run the circling year,
The clouds drop fatness, & the fruits appear,
Thee as the Lord of all below he plac'd,
Free in thy choice, & by thy chusing bless'd,
Tis true we must account for all we do,
But to a God alone th' account is due.
Gently awhile sweet Breezes move along,
Then swiftly bear aloft my rising song.

The Seraphim, & all the Heavenly pow'r,
Bright in their shapes, but in their virtues more,
Came to the shade where our first parents lay,
They heard him reason, & they heard her pray,
Then struck their Golden harps, & as they flew,
Cry'd, Halelujah, man is made for heaven too.
Go on, my Muse, Go on, & Gratefully express,
The Creatures thanks, in the Creators praise.

To see this pair the fallen powrs came in,
Torturd with malice, & deformd by sin,
They saw this happy pair designd to fill
The realms, from whence they fell by doing ill,
They heard their Joyfull anthems to their God,
& faign they woud have harmd ym if they coud,
Whom they woud harm they impotently curse,
Their strength indeed was great but God was ours.
Go on, My Muse, Go on, & Gratefully express.
The Creatures thanks, in the Creators praise.

I know I cannot speak his mercy's through,
Yet what I can, of what I ought Ile do,
Mean as they are, my notes to him belong,
Mean as it is, he will reward my song.
Go on, my Muse go on, & gratefully express
The Creatures thanks, in the Creators praise.

On such a theam I coud for ever dwell,
Thus lett my voice when I must perish fail
& thus my monument my story tell;
Here lyes a Youth—stay passenger & pray,
Nor pitty him who di'd no common way,
But when his breath was all in hymns bestowd
Sent up his soul to bear 'em to his God.

So lett me end, the twilight does appear,
The heat has left to rarify the air,
The winds it broke grow strong enough to fly,
Yes swiftly fly ye winds, & bear my Lays on high.

Hezekiah

From the bleak Beach and broad expanse of sea,
To lofty Salem, Thought direct thy way;
Mount thy light chariot, move along the plains,
And end thy flight where Hezekiah reigns.

How swiftly thought has pass'd from land to land,
And quite outrun Time's meas'ring glass of sand,
Great Salem's walls appear and I resort
To view the state of Hezekiah's court.

Well may that king a pious verse inspire,
Who cleans'd the temple, who reviv'd the choir,
Pleas'd with the service David fix'd before,
That heav'nly musick might on earth adore.
Deep-rob'd in white, he made the Levites stand

With Cymbals, Harps, and Psaltries in their hand;
He gave the Priests their trumpets, prompt to raise
The tuneful soul, by force of sound to praise.
A skilful master for the song he chose,
The songs were David's these, and Asaph's those.
Then burns their off'ring, all around rejoice,
Each tunes his instrument to join the voice;
The trumpets sounded, and the singers sung,
The People worship'd and the temple rung.
Each while the victim burns presents his heart,
Then the Priest blesses, and the People part.

Hail sacred musick! since you know to draw
The soul to Heav'n, the spirit to the law,
I come to prove thy force, thy warbling string
May tune my soul to write what others sing.

But is this Salem? this the proms'd bliss,
These sighs and groans? what means the realm by this?
What solemn sorrow dwells in ev'ry street?
What fear confounds the downcast looks I meet?
Alas the King! whole nations sink with woe,
When righteous Kings are summon'd hence to go;
The King lies sick, and thus to speak his doom,
The Prophet, grave Isaiah, stalks the room:
Oh Prince thy servant sent from God, believe,
Set all in order for thou can'st not live.
Solemn he said, and sighing left the place,
Deep prints of horror furrow'd ev'ry face,
Within their minds appear eternal glooms,
Black gaping marbles of their monarchs tombs,
A King belov'd deceas'd, his offspring none,
And wars destructive e'er they fix the throne.
Strait to the wall he turn'd with dark despair,
('Twas tow'rds the temple, or for private pray'r,)
And thus to God the pious monarch spoke,
Who burn'd the groves, the brazen serpent broke:
Remember Lord with what a heart for right,
What care for truth, I walk'd within thy sight.

'Twas thus with terror, pray'rs and tears he toss'd,
When the mid-court the grave Isaiah cross'd,
Whom in the cedar columns of the square,
Meets a sweet Angel hung in glitt'ring air.
Seiz'd with a trance he stop'd, before his eye
Clears a rais'd arch of visionary sky,
Where as a minute pass'd, the greater light
Purpling appear'd, and south'd and set in night;
A Moon succeeding leads the starry train,
She glides, and sinks her silver horns again:
A second fanci'd morning drives the shades;

Clos'd by the dark the second ev'ning fades;
The third bright dawn awakes, and strait he sees
The temple rise, the monarch on his knees.
Pleas'd with the scene, his inward thoughts rejoice,
When thus the Guardian angel form'd a voice.
Now tow'rds the captain of my people go,
And, Seer, relate him what thy visions show,
The Lord has heard his words, and seen his tears,
And through fifteen extends his future years.

Here to the room prepar'd with dismal black,
The Prophet turning, brought the comfort back.
Oh monarch hail, he cry'd, thy words are heard,
Thy virtuous actions meet a kind regard,
God gives thee fifteen years, when thrice a day,
Shews the round Sun, within the temple pray.

When thrice the day! surpriz'd the monarch cries,
When thrice the Sun! what pow'r have I to rise!
But if thy comfort's human or divine,
'Tis short to prove it—give thy prince a sign.

Behold, the Prophet cry'd, (and stretch'd his hands)
Against yon lattice where the dial stands,
Now shall the Sun a backward journey go
Through ten drawn lines, or leap to ten below.
'Tis easier posting nature's airy track,
Replies the monarch, let the Sun go back.
Attentive here he gaz'd, the prophet pray'd,
Back went the Sun, and back pursu'd the shade.

Chear'd by the sign, and by the Prophet heal'd,
What sacred thanks his gratitude reveal'd?
As sickly Swallows when a summer ends,
Who miss'd the passage with their flying friends,
Take to a wall, there lean the languid head,
While all who find them think the sleepers dead;
If yet their warmth new days of summer bring,
They wake and joyful flutter up to sing;
So far'd the monarch, sick to death he lay,
His court despair'd, and watch'd the last decay;
At length new favour shines, new life he gains,
And rais'd he sings; 'tis thus the song remains.

I said, my God, when in the loath'd disease
Thy Prophet's words cut off my future days,
Now to the grave with mournful haste I go,
Now death unbars his sable gates below.
How might my years by course of nature last?
But thou pronounc'd it, and the prospect pass'd.
I said, my God, thy servant now no more

Shall in thy Temple's sacred courts adore,
No more on earth with living man converse,
Shrunk in a cold uncomfortable hearse.
My life, like tents which wand'ring shepherds raise,
Proves a short dwelling and removes at ease.
My sins pursue me, see the deadly band,
My God, who sees them, cuts me from the land;
As when a weaver finds his labour sped,
Swift from the beam he parts the fast'ning thread.
With pining sickness all from night to day,
From day to night, he makes my strength decay:
Reck'ning the time, I roll with restless groans,
'Till with a lion's force, he crush my bones,
New-morning dawns, but like the morning past,
'Tis day, 'tis night, and still my sorrows last.
Now screaming like the Crane my words I spoke,
Now like the swallow, chatt'ring quick and broke,
Now like the doleful dove, when on the plains
Her mourning tone affects the list'ning swains.
To heav'n for aid my wearying eyes I throw,
At length they're weary'd quite, and sink with woe.
From death's arrest for some delays I sue,
Thou Lord who judg'd me, thou reprieve me too.

Rapture of joy! what can thy servant say?
He sent his Prophet to prolong my day;
Through my glad Limbs I feel the wonder run,
Thus said the Lord, and this Himself has done.
Soft shall I walk, and well secur'd from fears
Possess the comforts of my future years.
Keep soft my heart, keep humble while they roll,
Nor e'er forget my bitterness of soul.
'Tis by the means thy sacred words supply
That mankind live, but in peculiar I;
A second grant thy mercy pleas'd to give,
And my rais'd spirits doubly seem to live.
Behold the time! when peace adorn'd my reign,
'Twas then I felt my stroke of humbling pain;
Corruption dug her pit, I fear'd to sink,
God lov'd my soul, and snatch'd me from the brink.
He turn'd my follies from his gracious eye,
As men who pass accounts and cast them by.

What mouth has death which can thy praise proclaim?
What tongue the grave to speak thy glorious name?
Or will the senseless dead exult with mirth,
Mov'd to their hope by promises on earth?
The living Lord, the living only praise,
The living only fit to sing thy lays,
These feel thy favours, these thy temple see,
These raise the song, as I this day to thee.

Nor will thy truth the present only reach,
This the good fathers shall their offspring teach,
Report the blessings which adorn my page,
And hand their own with mine from age to age.

So when the Maker heard his creature crave,
So kindly rose his ready Will to save.
Then march we solemn tow'rds the Temple door,
While all our joyful musick sounds before,
There on this day through all my life appear,
When this comes round in each returning year,
There strike the strings, our voices jointly raise,
And let his dwellings hear my songs of praise.

Thus wrote the monarch, and I'll think the lay
Design'd for publick when he went to pray;
I'll think the perfect composition runs,
Perform'd by Heman's or Jeduthun's sons.

Then since the time arrives the Seer foretold,
And the third morning rolls an orb of gold,
With thankful zeal recover'd prince prepare
To lead thy nation to the Dome of pray'r.

My fancy takes her chariot once again,
Moves the rich wheels, and mingles in thy train;
She sees the singers reach Moriah's hill,
The minstrels follow, then the porches fill,
She wakes the num'rous instruments of art,
That each perform its own adapted part,
Seeks airs expressive of thy grateful strains,
And list'ning hears the vary'd tune she feigns.

From a grave pitch, to speak the Monarch's woe,
The notes flow down and deeply sound below,
All long-continuing, while depriv'd of ease
He rolls for tedious nights and heavy days.
Here intermix'd with discord, when the Crane
Screams in the notes through sharper sense of pain;
There run with descant on, and taught to shake
When pangs repeated force the voice to break;
Now like the dove they murmur, 'till in sighs
They fall, and languish with the failing eyes.
Then slowly slack'ning, to surprize the more,
From a dead pause, his exclamations soar,
To meet brisk health the notes ascending fly,
Live with the living, and exult on high.
Yet still distinct in parts the musick plays,
'Till prince and people both are call'd to praise,
Then all uniting strongly strike the string,
Put forth their utmost breath, and loudly sing;

The wide spread chorus fills the sacred ground,
And holy transport scales the clouds with sound.

Or thus, or livelier, if their hand and voice
Join'd the good anthem, might the realm rejoice.

This story known, the learn'd Chaldeans came,
Drawn by the sign observ'd, or mov'd by fame;
These ask the fact for Hezekiah done,
And much they wonder at their God the sun,
That thrice he drove through one extent of day
His gold-shod horses in etherial way:
Then vainly ground their guess on nature's laws,
The soundest knowledge owns a greater cause.

Faith knows the fact transcends, and bids me find
What help for practice here incites the mind;
Strait to the song, the thankful song I move,
May such the voice of ev'ry creature prove,
If ev'ry creature meets its share of woe,
And for kind rescues ev'ry creature owe;
In publick so thy Maker's praise proclaim,
Nor what you beg'd with tears, conceal with shame.

'Tis there the ministry thy name repeat
And tell what mercies were vouchsaf'd of late,
Then joins the church, and begs through all our days
Not only with our lips, but lives to praise.

'Tis there our Sov'reigns for a signal day,
The feast proclaim'd, their signal thanks repay.
O'er the long streets we see the chariots wheel,
And, following, think of Hezekiah still;
In the bless'd Dome we meet the white-rob'd Choir,
In whose sweet notes our ravish'd souls aspire;
Side answ'ring side we hear and bear a part,
All warm'd with language from the grateful heart,
Or raise the song where meeting keys rejoice,
And teach the Base to wed the treble voice;
Arts soft'ning ecchos in the musick sound,
And answ'ring natures from the roof rebound.

Here close my verse, the service asks no more,
Bless thy good God, and give the transport o'er.

Once Pope Under Jevais Resolvd to Adventure

Once Pope under Jevais resolvd to adventure
& from a Good Poet Pope turnd an ill painter

So from a Good Painter Charles Jervais we hope
May turn an ill Poet by living with Pope
Then Each may perform the true parts of a friend
While each will have something to blame or commend

To praise, and still with just respect to praise
A Bard triumphant in immortal bays,
The Learn'd to show, the Sensible commend,
Yet still preserve the province of the Friend,
What life, what vigour must the lines require?
What Music tune them, what affection fire?

O might thy Genius in my bosom shine!
Thou should'st not fail of numbers worthy thine;
The brightest Ancients might at once agree,
To sing within my lays, and sing of thee.

Horace himself wou'd own thou dost excell
In candid arts to play the Critic well.
Ovid himself might wish to sing the Dame,
Whom Windsor-Forest sees a gliding stream:
On silver feet, with annual Osier crown'd,
She runs for ever thro' Poetic ground.

How flame the glories of Belinda's Hair,
Made by thy Muse the envy of the Fair?
Less shone the tresses Ægypt's Princess wore,
Which sweet Callimachus so sung before.
Here courtly trifles set the world at odds;
Belles war with Beaus, and Whims descend for Gods.
The new Machines, in names of ridicule,
Mock the grave frenzy of the Chimick fool.
But know, ye fair, a point conceal'd with art,
The Sylphs and Gnomes are but a woman's heart.
The Graces stand in sight; a Satyr-train,
Peeps o'er their head, and laughs behind the scene.

In Fame's fair Temple o'er the boldest wits,
Inshrin'd on high, the sacred Virgil sits,
And sits in measures, such as Virgil's Muse,
To place thee near him, might be fond to chuse.
How might he tune th' alternate reed with thee,
Perhaps a Strephon thou, a Daphnis he;
While some old Damon, o'er the vulgar wise,
Thinks he deserves, and thou deserv'st the Prize.
Rapt with the thought, my fancy seeks the plains,
And turns me shepherd while I hear the strains.

Indulgent nurse of ev'ry tender gale,
Parent of flowrets, old Arcadia hail!
Here in the cool my limbs at ease I spread,
Here let thy Poplars whisper o'er my head!
Still slide thy waters soft among the trees,
Thy Aspins quiver in a breathing breeze!
Smile, all ye valleys, in eternal spring,
Be hush'd, ye winds! while Pope and Virgil sing.

In English lays, and all sublimely great,
Thy Homer warms with all his ancient heat;
He shines in Council, thunders in the fight,
And flames with ev'ry sense of great delight.
Long has that Poet reign'd, and long unknown,
Like Monarchs sparkling on a distant throne;
In all the majesty of Greek retir'd,
Himself unknown, his mighty name admir'd;
His language failing, wrapt him round with night;
Thine, rais'd by thee, recalls the work to light.
So wealthy Mines, that ages long before
Fed the large realms around with golden Oar,
When choak'd by sinking banks, no more appear,
And shepherds only say, The mines were here:
Should some rich youth (if nature warm his heart,
And all his projects stand inform'd with art)
Here clear the caves, there ope the leading vein;
The mines detected flame with gold again.

How vast, how copious are thy new designs!
How ev'ry Music varies in thy lines!
Still, as I read, I feel my bosom beat,
And rise in raptures by another's heat.
Thus in the wood, when summer dress'd the days,
When Windsor lent us tuneful hours of ease,
Our ears the lark, the thrush, the turtle blest,
And Philomela sweetest o'er the rest:
The shades resound with song—O softly tread,
While a whole season warbles round my head.

This to my friend—and when a friend inspires,
My silent harp its master's hand requires,
Shakes off the dust, and makes these rocks resound;
For fortune plac'd me in unfertile ground.
Far from the joys that with my soul agree,
From wit, from learning—very far from thee.
Here moss-grown trees expand the smallest leaf;
Here half an Acre's corn is half a sheaf;
Here hills with naked heads the tempest meet,
Rocks at their sides, and torrents at their feet;
Or lazy lakes, unconscious of a flood,
Whose dull, brown Naiads ever sleep in mud.

Yet here Content can dwell, and learned ease,
A Friend delight me, and an Author please;
Ev'n here I sing, when Pope supplies the theme,
Shew my own love, tho' not increase his fame.

I Lookd & In A Moment Run

I look & in a moment run
The poison thro' my veins
Nor Celia think your self too young
To give me amorous pains
When heaven did the Sun create
He shone as bright as now
& wth the fires which guild them yet
The infant starrs did glow.

On Ye Plott Against King William

Rome when she could King Pyrrhus Life have bought
She scornd a triumph So ignobly gott,
The treason & ye traitor both disdaind,
& ever Justly conquerd ever Justly reignd.
But (Like an Affrick) England serpents bears
Which would their parent country's bowels teare,
Our better Genius tumble Headlong down,
& sett our evil one upon ye throne.
The Titans wickedness nere reacht so high,
They fought but for ye empire of ye sky,
When Jove unjustly held the soveraignity.
That Godlike soul which doth inform our state
Gerion-like, ye'de conquer by deceit.
Ye in one stroke would make three kingdomes bleed,
& Leave our Iles as nile without a head.
Cease fooles with Hellish plotts to wrack your brain,
Ye Cannot wound a God, ye strive in vain;
Ixions fate again is acted here,
He for a Deity imbrac't, ye wounded, air.

Chloris Appearing In A Looking Glass

Oft have I seen a Piece of Art,
Of Light and Shade, the Mixture fine,
Speak all the Passions of the Heart,
And shew true Life in every Line.
But what is this before my Eyes,
With every Feature, every Grace,
That strikes with Love and with Surprize,

And gives me all the Vital Face.
It is not Chloris, for behold
The shifting Phantom comes and goes;
And when 'tis here 'tis pale and cold,
Nor any Female Softness knows.
But 'tis her Image, for I feel
The very Pains that Chloris gives;
Her Charms are there, I know 'em well,
I see what in my Bosom lives.
Oh cou'd I but the Picture save!
'Tis drawn by her own matchless Skill;
Nature the lively Colours gave,
And she need only Look to Kill.
Ah! Fair-one, will it not suffice,
That I shou'd once, your Victim lye;
Unless you multiply your Eyes,
And strive to make me doubly Dye.

Hark The Thundring Drums Inviting

Hark the thundring Drums inviting
All our forward youth to arms
Hark the trumpets sounds exciting
Manly Soules with fierce alarms
Peace affords an Idle pleasure
Glory shines an active flame
Life has but too short a Measure
Strive to make it long by fame.
See the brave by boldly daring
Raises trophys of the slain
See the brave by nothing fearing
Comes in triumph back again
The Men admire the Women love him
Fortune favours all he does
The Powrs that bless the great approve him
Praise & Lawrell crown his brows.

When Ore My Temples Balmy Vapours Rise

When ore my temples balmy vapours rise
Whose soft suffusion dims the sinking eyes
Gay dreams in troops fantastically light
On silent plumes wave down through sable night
Nights sable curtains draw before my eye
gently clears a visionary Sky
the running darkness draws its dusky shade
from off the beautys of a flowry mead
More still more forsakes the lengthening plain

Mounts gray ends it in a sylvan scene.

Poizd & aloft I sail in glittring air
Joy to view my newborn earth so fair

Young Philomela's Powrfull Dart

Young Philomela's powrfull dart
Two gentle shepheard's hitt
With Beauty touchd Amintors heart
Celadons with witt
The Rivall swains on either side
Their am'rous pangs expressd
Till young Amintor she denyd
Celadon she blessd
The youth who mett a mutuall fire
In pleasure lost his pain
The others hopeless flames expire
Beneath a cold disdain
Ye Priests of love ye Poets tell
What Cupids forces are
If when the suit goes ill or well
No more we serve a fair.

Homer's Battle Of The Frogs And Mice. Book I

Names of the Mice.
Psycarpax, One who plunders Granaries.
Troxartas, A Bread-eater.
Lychomile, A Licker of Meal.
Pternotractas, A Bacon-eater.
Lychopinax, A Licker of Dishes.
Embasichytros, A Creeper into Pots.
Lychenor, A Name from Licking.
Troglodytes, One who runs into Holes.
Artophagus, Who feeds on Bread.
Tyroglyphus, A Cheese-Scooper.
Pternoglyphus, A Bacon-Scooper.
Pternophagus, A Bacon-Eater.
Cnissodioctes, One who follows the Steam of Kitchens.
Sitophagus, An Eater of Wheat.
Meridarpax, One who plunders his Share.

Names of the Frogs.
Physignathus, One who swells his Cheeks.
Peleus, A Name from Mud.
Hydromeduse, A Ruler in the Waters.

Hypsiboas, A loud Bawler.
Pelion, From Mud.
Seutlæus, Call'd from the Beets.
Polyphonus, A great Babbler.
Lymnocharis, One who loves the Lake.
Crambophagus, Cabbage-eater.
Lymnisius, Call'd from the Lake.
Calaminthius, From the Herb.
Hydrocharis, Who loves the Water.
Borborocates, Who lies in the Mud.
Prassophagus, An Eater of Garlick.
Pelusius, From Mud.
Pelobates, Who walks in the Dirt.
Prassæus, Call'd from Garlick.
Craugasides, from Croaking.

To fill my rising Song with sacred Fire,
Ye tuneful Nine, ye sweet Celestial Quire!
From Helicon's imbow'ring Height repair,
Attend my Labours, and reward my Pray'r.
The dreadful Toils of raging Mars I write,
The Springs of Contest, and the Fields of Fight;
How threatning Mice advanc'd with warlike Grace,
And wag'd dire Combats with the croaking Race.
Not louder Tumults shook Olympus' Tow'rs,
When Earth-born Giants dar'd Immortal Pow'rs.
These equal Acts an equal Glory claim,
And thus the Muse records the Tale of Fame.

Once on a Time, fatigu'd and out of Breath,
And just escap'd the stretching Claws of Death,
A Gentle Mouse, whom Cats pursu'd in vain,
Flies swift-of-foot across the neighb'ring Plain,
Hangs o'er a Brink, his eager Thirst to cool,
And dips his Whiskers in the standing Pool;
When near a courteous Frog advanc'd his Head,
And from the Waters, hoarse-resounding said,

What art thou, Stranger? What the Line you boast?
What Chance hath cast thee panting on our Coast?
With strictest Truth let all thy Words agree,
Nor let me find a faithless Mouse in thee.
If worthy Friendship, proffer'd Friendship take,
And entring view the pleasurable Lake:
Range o'er my Palace, in my Bounty share,
And glad return from hospitable Fare.
This Silver Realm extends beneath my Sway,
And me, their Monarch, all its Frogs obey.
Great Physignathus I, from Peleus' Race,
Begot in fair Hydromeduse' Embrace,

Where by the nuptial Bank that paints his Side,
The swift Eridanus delights to glide.
Thee too, thy Form, thy Strength, and Port proclaim,
A scepter'd King; a Son of Martial Fame;
Then trace thy Line, and aid my guessing Eyes.
Thus ceas'd the Frog, and thus the Mouse replies.

Known to the Gods, the Men, the Birds that fly
Thro' wild Expanses of the midway Sky,
My Name resounds; and if unknown to thee,
The Soul of Great Psycarpax lives in me.
Of brave Troxartas' Line, whose sleeky Down
In Love compress'd Lychomile the brown.
My Mother she, and Princess of the Plains
Where-e're her Father Pternotroctas reigns:
Born where a Cabin lifts its airy Shed,
With Figs, with Nuts, with vary'd Dainties fed.
But since our Natures nought in common know,
From what Foundation can a Friendship grow?
These curling Waters o'er thy Palace roll;
But Man's high Food supports my Princely Soul.
In vain the circled Loaves attempt to lie
Conceal'd in Flaskets from my curious Eye,
In vain the Tripe that boasts the whitest Hue,
In vain the gilded Bacon shuns my View,
In vain the Cheeses, Offspring of the Pale,
Or honey'd Cakes, which Gods themselves regale.
And as in Arts I shine, in Arms I fight,
Mix'd with the bravest, and unknown to Flight.
Tho' large to mine the humane Form appear,
Not Man himself can smite my Soul with Fear.
Sly to the Bed with silent Steps I go,
Attempt his Finger, or attack his Toe,
And fix indented Wounds with dext'rous Skill,
Sleeping he feels, and only seems to feel.
Yet have we Foes which direful Dangers cause,
Grim Owls with Talons arm'd, and Cats with Claws,
And that false Trap, the Den of silent Fate,
Where Death his Ambush plants around the Bait;
All-dreaded these, and dreadful o'er the rest
The potent Warriours of the tabby Vest,
If to the dark we fly, the Dark they trace,
And rend our Heroes of the nibling Race.
But me, nor Stalks, nor watrish Herbs delight,
Nor can the crimson Radish charm my Sight,
The Lake-resounding Frogs selected Fare,
Which not a Mouse of any Tast can bear.

As thus the downy Prince his Mind exprest,
His Answer thus the croaking King addrest.

Thy Words luxuriant on thy Dainties rove,
And, stranger, we can boast of bounteous Jove:
We sport in Water, or we dance on Land,
And born amphibious, Food from both command.
But trust thy self where Wonders ask thy View,
And safely tempt those Seas, I'll bear thee through:
Ascend my Shoulders, firmly keep thy Seat,
And reach my marshy Court, and feast in State.

He said, and leant his Back; with nimble Bound
Leaps the light Mouse, and clasps his Arms around,
Then wond'ring floats, and sees with glad Survey
The winding Banks dissemble Ports at Sea.
But when aloft the curling Water rides,
And wets with azure Wave his downy Sides,
His Thoughts grow conscious of approaching Woe,
His idle Tears with vain Repentance flow,
His Locks he rends, his trembling Feet he rears,
Thick beats his Heart with unaccustom'd Fears;
He sighs, and chill'd with Danger, longs for Shore:
His Tail extended forms a fruitless Oar,
Half-drench'd in liquid Death his Pray'rs he spake,
And thus bemoan'd him from the dreadful Lake.

So pass'd Europa thro' the rapid Sea,
Trembling and fainting all the vent'rous Way;
With oary Feet the Bull triumphant rode,
And safe in Crete depos'd his lovely Load.
Ah safe at last! may thus the Frog support
My trembling Limbs to reach his ample Court.

As thus he sorrows, Death ambiguous grows,
Lo! from the deep a Water-Hydra rose;
He rolls his sanguin'd Eyes, his Bosom heaves,
And darts with active Rage along the Waves.
Confus'd, the Monarch sees his hissing Foe,
And dives to shun the sable Fates below.
Forgetful Frog! The Friend thy Shoulders bore,
Unskill'd in Swimming, floats remote from Shore.
He grasps with fruitless Hands to find Relief,
Supinely falls, and grinds his Teeth with Grief,
Plunging he sinks, and struggling mounts again,
And sinks, and strives, but strives with Fate in vain.
The weighty Moisture clogs his hairy Vest,
And thus the Prince his dying Rage exprest.

Nor thou, that flings me flound'ring from thy Back,
As from hard Rocks rebounds the shatt'ring Wrack,
Nor thou shalt 'scape thy Due, perfidious King!
Pursu'd by Vengeance on the swiftest Wing:
At Land thy Strength could never equal mine,

At Sea to conquer, and by Craft, was thine.
But Heav'n has Gods, and Gods have searching Eyes:
Ye Mice, ye Mice, my great Avengers rise!

This said, he sighing gasp'd, and gasping dy'd.
His Death the young Lychopinax espy'd,
As on the flow'ry Brink he pass'd the Day,
Bask'd in the Beams, and loyter'd Life away:
Loud shrieks the Mouse, his Shrieks the Shores repeat;
The nibbling Nation learn their Heroe's Fate:
Grief, dismal Grief ensues; deep Murmur's sound,
And shriller Fury fills the deafen'd Ground;
From Lodge to Lodge the sacred Heralds run,
To fix their Council with the rising Sun;
Where great Troxartas crown'd in Glory reigns,
And winds his length'ning Court beneath the Plains;
Psycarpax Father, Father now no more!
For poor Psycarpax lies remote from Shore;
Supine he lies! the silent Waters stand,
And no kind Billow wafts the Dead to Land!

Homer's Battle Of The Frogs And Mice. Book II

When rosy-finger'd Morn had ting'd the Clouds,
Around their Monarch-Mouse the Nation crouds,
Slow rose the Monarch, heav'd his anxious Breast,
And thus, the Council fill'd with Rage, addrest.

For lost Psycarpax much my Soul endures,
'Tis mine the private Grief, the publick, yours.
Three warlike Sons adorn'd my nuptial Bed,
Three Sons, alas, before their Father dead!
Our Eldest perish'd by the rav'ning Cat,
As near my Court the Prince unheedful sate.
Our next, an Engine fraught with Danger drew,
The Portal gap'd, the Bait was hung in View,
Dire Arts assist the Trap, the Fates decoy,
And Men unpitying kill'd my gallant Boy!
The last, his Country's Hope, his Parent's Pride,
Plung'd in the Lake by Physignathus, dy'd.
Rouse all the War, my Friends! avenge the Deed,
And bleed that Monarch, and his Nation bleed.

His Words in ev'ry Breast inspir'd Alarms,
And careful Mars supply'd their Host with Arms.
In verdant Hulls despoil'd of all their Beans,
The buskin'd Warriours stalk'd along the Plains,
Quills aptly bound, their bracing Corselet made,
Fac'd with the Plunder of a Cat they flay'd,

The Lamp's round Boss affords their ample Shield,
Large Shells of Nuts their cov'ring Helmet yield;
And o'er the Region, with reflected Rays,
Tall Groves of Needles for their Lances blaze.
Dreadful in Arms the marching Mice appear:
The wond'ring Frogs perceive the Tumult near,
Forsake the Waters, thick'ning form a Ring,
And ask, and hearken, whence the Noises spring;
When near the Croud, disclos'd to publick View,
The valiant Chief Embasichytros drew:
The sacred Herald's Scepter grac'd his Hand,
And thus his Words exprest his King's Command.

Ye Frogs! the Mice with Vengeance fir'd, advance,
And deckt in Armour shake the shining Lance;
Their hapless Prince by Physignathus slain,
Extends incumbent on the watry Plain.
Then arm your Host, the doubtful Battle try;
Lead forth those Frogs that have the Soul to die.

The Chief retires, the Crowd the Challenge hear,
And proudly-swelling, yet perplex'd appear,
Much they resent, yet much their Monarch blame,
Who rising, spoke to clear his tainted Fame.

O Friends, I never forc'd the Mouse to Death,
Nor saw the Gaspings of his latest Breath.
He, vain of Youth, our Art of Swimming try'd,
And vent'rous, in the Lake the Wanton dy'd.
To Vengeance now by false Appearance led,
They point their Anger at my guiltless Head.
But wage the rising War by deep Device,
And turn its Fury on the crafty Mice.
Your King directs the Way; my Thoughts elate
With Hopes of Conquest, form Designs of Fate.
Where high the Banks their verdant Surface heave,
And the steep Sides confine the sleeping Wave,
There, near the Margin, and in Armour bright,
Sustain the first impetuous Shocks of Fight:
Then where the dancing Feather joins the Crest,
Let each brave Frog his obvious Mouse arrest;
Each strongly grasping, headlong plunge a Foe,
'Till countless Circles whirl the Lake below;
Down sink the Mice in yielding Waters drown'd;
Loud flash the Waters; ecchoing Shores resound:
The Frogs triumphant tread the conquer'd Plain,
And raise their glorious Trophies of the slain.

He spake no more, his prudent Scheme imparts
Redoubling Ardour to the boldest Hearts.
Green was the Suit his arming Heroes chose,

Around their Legs the Greaves of Mallows close,
Green were the Beetes about their Shoulders laid,
And green the Colewort, which the Target made.
Form'd of the vary'd Shells the Waters yield,
Their glossy Helmets glist'ned o'er the Field;
And tap'ring Sea-Reeds for the polish'd Spear,
With upright Order pierc'd the ambient Air.
Thus dress'd for War, they take th' appointed Height,
Poize the long Arms, and urge the promis'd Fight.

But now, where Jove's irradiate Spires arise,
With Stars surrounded in Æthereal Skies,
(A Solemn Council call'd) the brazen Gates
Unbar; the Gods assume their golden Seats:
The Sire superiour leans, and points to show
What wond'rous Combats Mortals wage below:
How strong, how large, the num'rous Heroes stride;
What Length of Lance they shake with warlike Pride:
What eager Fire, their rapid March reveals;
So the fierce Centaurs ravag'd o'er the Dales;
And so confirm'd, the daring Titans rose,
Heap'd Hills on Hills, and bid the Gods be Foes.

This seen, the Pow'r his sacred Visage rears,
He casts a pitying Smile on worldly Cares,
And asks what heav'nly Guardians take the List,
Or who the Mice, or who the Frogs assist?

Then thus to Pallas. If my Daughter's Mind
Have join'd the Mice, why stays she still behind?
Drawn forth by sav'ry Steams they wind their Way,
And sure Attendance round thine Altar pay,
Where while the Victims gratify their Tast,
They sport to please the Goddess of the Feast.

Thus spake the Ruler of the spacious Skies,
When thus, resolv'd, the Blue-Ey'd Maid replies.
In vain, my Father! all their Dangers plead,
To such, thy Pallas never grants her Aid.
My flow'ry Wreaths they petulantly spoil,
And rob my chrystal Lamps of feeding Oil.
(Ills following Ills) but what afflicts me more,
My Veil, that idle Race profanely tore.
The Web was curious, wrought with Art divine;
Relentless Wretches! all the Work was mine.
Along the Loom the purple Warp I spread,
Cast the light Shoot, and crost the silver Thread;
In this their Teeth a thousand Breaches tear,
The thousand Breaches skilful Hands repair,
For which vile earthly Dunns thy Daughter grieve,
And Gods, that use no Coin, have none to give.

And Learning's Goddess never less can owe,
Neglected Learning gets no Wealth below.
Nor let the Frogs to gain my Succour sue,
Those clam'rous Fools have lost my Favour too.
For late, when all the Conflict ceast at Night,
When my stretch'd Sinews work'd with eager Fight,
When spent with glorious Toil, I left the Field,
And sunk for Slumber on my swelling Shield,
Lo from the Deep, repelling sweet Repose,
With noisy Croakings half the Nation rose:
Devoid of Rest, with aking Brows I lay,
'Till Cocks proclaim'd the crimson Dawn of Day.
Let all, like me, from either Host forbear,
Nor tempt the flying Furies of the Spear.
Let heav'nly Blood (or what for Blood may flow)
Adorn the Conquest of a meaner Foe,
Who, wildly rushing, meet the wond'rous Odds,
Tho' Gods oppose, and brave the wounded Gods.
O'er gilded Clouds reclin'd, the Danger view,
And be the Wars of Mortals Scenes for you.

So mov'd the blue-ey'd Queen, her Words persuade,
Great Jove assented, and the rest obey'd.

Homer's Battle Of The Frogs And Mice. Book III

Now Front to Front the marching Armies shine,
Halt e'er they meet, and form the length'ning Line,
The Chiefs conspicuous seen, and heard afar,
Give the loud Sign to loose the rushing War;
Their dreadful Trumpets deep-mouth'd Hornets sound,
The sounded Charge remurmurs o'er the Ground,
Ev'n Jove proclaims a Field of Horror nigh,
And rolls low Thunder thro' the troubled Sky.

First to the Fight the large Hypsiboas flew,
And brave Lychenor with a Javelin slew.
The luckless Warriour fill'd with gen'rous Flame,
Stood foremost glitt'ring in the Post of Fame;
When in his Liver struck, the Jav'lin hung;
The Mouse fell thund'ring, and the Target rung;
Prone to the Ground he sinks his closing Eye,
And soil'd in Dust his lovely Tresses lie.
A Spear at Pelion Troglodytes cast,
The missive Spear within the Bosom past;
Death's sable Shades the fainting Frog surround,
And Life's red Tide runs ebbing from the Wound.
Embasichytros felt Seutlæus' Dart
Transfix, and quiver in his panting Heart;

But great Artophagus aveng'd the slain,
And big Seutlæus tumbling loads the Plain,
And Polyphonus dies, a Frog renown'd,
For boastful Speech and Turbulence of Sound;
Deep thro' the Belly pierc'd, supine he lay,
And breath'd his Soul against the Face of Day.
The strong Lymnocharis, who view'd with Ire,
A Victor triumph, and a Friend expire;
And fiercely flung where Troglodytes fought,
With heaving Arms a rocky Fragment caught,
A Warriour vers'd in Arts, of sure Retreat,
Yet Arts in vain elude impending Fate;
Full on his sinewy Neck the Fragment fell,
And o'er his Eye-lids Clouds eternal dwell.
Lychenor (second of the glorious Name)
Striding advanc'd, and took no wand'ring Aim;
Thro' all the Frog the shining Jav'lin flies,
And near the vanquish'd Mouse the Victor dies;
The dreadful Stroke Crambophagus affrights,
Long bred to Banquets, less inur'd to Fights,
Heedless he runs, and stumbles o'er the Steep,
And wildly flound'ring flashes up the Deep;
Lychenor following with a downward Blow
Reach'd in the Lake his unrecover'd Foe;
Gasping he rolls, a purple Stream of Blood
Distains the Surface of the Silver Flood;
Thro' the wide Wound the rushing Entrails throng,
And slow the breathless Carkass floats along.
Lymnisius good Tyroglyphus assails,
Prince of the Mice that haunt the flow'ry Vales,
Lost to the milky Fares and rural Seat,
He came to perish on the Bank of Fate.
The dread Pternoglyphus demands the Fight,
Which tender Calaminthius shuns by Flight,
Drops the green Target, springing quits the Foe,
Glides thro' the Lake, and safely dives below.
The dire Pternophagus divides his Way
Thro' breaking Ranks, and leads the dreadful Day.
No nibbling Prince excell'd in Fierceness more,
His Parents fed him on the savage Boar;
But where his Lance the Field with Blood imbru'd,
Swift as he mov'd Hydrocharis pursu'd,
'Till fall'n in Death he lies, a shatt'ring Stone
Sounds on the Neck, and crushes all the Bone,
His Blood pollutes the Verdure of the Plain,
And from his Nostrils bursts the gushing Brain.
Lycopinax with Borbocætes fights
A blameless Frog, whom humbler Life delights;
The fatal Jav'lin unrelenting flies,
And Darkness seals the gentle Croaker's Eyes.
Incens'd Prassophagus with spritely Bound,

Bears Cnissiodortes off the rising Ground,
Then drags him o'er the Lake depriv'd of Breath,
And downward plunging, sinks his Soul to Death.
But now the great Psycarpax shines afar,
(Scarce he so great whose Loss provok'd the War)
Swift to revenge his fatal Jav'lin fled,
And thro' the Liver struck Pelusius dead;
His freckled Corps before the Victor fell,
His Soul indignant sought the Shades of Hell.
This saw Pelobates, and from the Flood
Lifts with both Hands a monst'rous Mass of Mud,
The Cloud obscene o'er all the Warrior flies,
Dishonours his brown Face, and blots his Eyes.
Enrag'd, and wildly sputtring, from the Shore
A Stone immense of Size the Warrior bore,
A Load for lab'ring Earth, whose Bulk to raise,
Asks ten degen'rate Mice of modern Days.
Full to the Leg arrives the crushing Wound,
The Frog supportless, wriths upon the Ground.
Thus flush'd, the Victor wars with matchless Force,
'Till loud Craugasides arrests his Course,
Hoarse-croaking Threats precede, with fatal Speed
Deep thro' the Belly runs the pointed Reed,
Then strongly tug'd, return'd imbru'd with Gore,
And on the Pile his reeking Entrails bore.
The lame Sitophagus oppress'd with Pain,
Creeps from the desp'rate Dangers of the Plain;
And where the Ditches rising Weeds supply,
To spread their lowly Shades beneath the Sky,
There lurks the silent Mouse reliev'd of Heat,
And safe imbower'd, avoids the Chance of Fate.
But here Troxartes, Physignathus there,
Whirl the dire Furies of the pointed Spear:
Then where the Foot around its Ankle plies,
Troxartes wounds, and Physignathus flies,
Halts to the Pool, a safe Retreat to find,
And trails a dangling Length of Leg behind.
The Mouse still urges, still the Frog retires,
And half in Anguish of the Flight expires;
Then pious Ardor young Prassæus brings,
Betwixt the Fortunes of contending Kings:
Lank, harmless Frog! with Forces hardly grown,
He darts the Reed in Combats not his own,
Which faintly tinkling on Troxartes' Shield,
Hangs at the Point, and drops upon the Field.

Now nobly tow'ring o'er the rest appears
A gallant Prince that far transcends his Years,
Pride of his Sire, and Glory of his House,
And more a Mars in Combat than a Mouse:
His Action bold, robust his ample Frame,

And Meridarpax his resounding Name.
The Warrior singled from the fighting Crowd,
Boasts the dire Honours of his Arms aloud;
Then strutting near the Lake, with Looks elate,
Threats all its Nations with approaching Fate.
And such his Strength, the Silver Lakes around,
Might roll their Waters o'er unpeopled Ground.
But pow'rful Jove who shews no less his Grace
To Frogs that perish, than to human Race,
Felt soft Compassion rising in his Soul,
And shook his sacred Head, that shook the Pole.
Then thus to all the gazing Pow'rs began,
The Sire of Gods, and Frogs, and Mouse, and Man.

What Seas of Blood I view, what Worlds of slain,
An Iliad rising from a Day's Campaign!
How fierce his Jav'lin o'er the trembling Lakes
The black-fur'd Hero Meridarpax shakes!
Unless some fav'ring Deity descend,
Soon will the Frogs loquacious Empire end.
Let dreadful Pallas wing'd with Pity fly,
And make her Ægis blaze before his Eye:
While Mars refulgent on his ratling Car,
Arrests his raging Rival of the War.

He ceas'd, reclining with attentive Head,
When thus the glorious God of Combats said.
Nor Pallas, Jove! tho' Pallas take the Field,
With all the Terrors of her hissing Shield,
Nor Mars himself, tho' Mars in Armour bright
Ascend his Car, and wheel amidst the Fight;
Nor these can drive the desp'rate Mouse afar,
And change the Fortunes of the bleeding War.
Let all go forth, all Heav'n in Arms arise,
Or launch thy own red Thunder from the Skies.
Such ardent Bolts as flew that wond'rous Day,
When Heaps of Titans mix'd with Mountains lay,
When all the Giant-Race enormous fell,
And huge Enceladus was hurl'd to Hell.

'Twas thus th' Armipotent advis'd the Gods,
When from his Throne the Cloud-Compeller nods,
Deep length'ning Thunders run from Pole to Pole,
Olympus trembles as the Thunders roll.
Then swift he whirls the brandish'd Bolt around,
And headlong darts it at the distant Ground,
The Bolt discharg'd inwrap'd with Light'ning flies,
And rends its flaming Passage thro' the Skies,
Then Earth's Inhabitants the Niblers shake,
And Frogs, the Dwellers in the Waters, quake.
Yet still the Mice advance their dread Design,

And the last Danger threats the croaking Line,
'Till Jove that inly mourn'd the Loss they bore,
With strange Assistants fill'd the frighted Shore.

Pour'd from the neighb'ring Strand, deform'd to View,
They march, a sudden unexpected Crew,
Strong Sutes of Armor round their Bodies close,
Which, like thick Anvils, blunt the force of Blows;
In wheeling Marches turn'd oblique they go,
With harpy Claws their Limbs divide below,
Fell Sheers the Passage to their Mouth command,
From out the Flesh the Bones by Nature stand,
Broad spread their Backs, their shining Shoulders rise,
Unnumber'd Joints distort their lengthen'd Thighs,
With nervous Cords their Hands are firmly brac'd,
Their round black Eye-balls in their Bosom plac'd,
On eight long Feet the wond'rous Warriors tread,
And either End alike supplies a Head.
These, mortal Wits to call the Crabs, agree;
The Gods have other Names for Things than we.

Now where the Jointures from their Loins depend,
The Heroes Tails with sev'ring Grasps they rend.
Here, short of Feet, depriv'd the Pow'r to fly,
There, without Hands upon the Field they lie.
Wrench'd from their Holds, and scatter'd all around,
The bended Lances heap the cumber'd Ground.
Helpless Amazement, Fear pursuing Fear,
And mad Confusion thro' their Host appear,
O'er the wild Wast with headlong Flight they go,
Or creep conceal'd in vaulted Holes below.

But down Olympus to the Western Seas,
Far-shooting Phœbus drove with fainter Rays,
And a whole War (so Jove ordain'd) begun,
Was fought, and ceas'd, in one revolving Sun.

On A Lady With A Foul Breath

Art thou alive? It cannot be,
There's so much Rottenness in Thee,
Corruption only is in Death;
And what's more Putrid than thy Breath?
Think not you Live, because you Speak,
For Graves such hollow Sounds can make;
And Respiration can't suffice,
For Vapours do from Caverns rise:
From Thee such noisom Stenches come,
Thy Mouth betrays thy Breast a Tomb.

Thy Body is a Corpse that goes,
By Magick rais'd from its Repose:
A Pestilence that walks by Day,
But falls at Night to Worms and Clay.
But I will to my Chloris run,
Who will not let me be undone:
The Sweets her Virgin-Breath contains,
Are fitted to remove my Pains;
There will I healing Nectar sip,
And to be sav'd, approach her Lip,
Tho' if I touch the matchless Dame,
I'm sure to burn with inward Flame.
Thus when I wou'd one Danger shun,
I'm strait upon another thrown:
I seek a Cure one Sore to ease,
Yet in that Cure's a New Disease.
But Love, tho' fatal, still can bless,
And greater Dangers hide the less;
I'll go where Passion bids me fly,
And chuse my Death, since I must Dye;
As Doves pursu'd by Birds of Prey,
Venture with milder Man to stay.

For Philip Ridgate Esq

To friend with fingers quick & limber,
I send this piece of tunefull timber:
that, as 'tis said in Orpheus story,
He may teach trees to dance a Bory;
Or else in modern Phrase more knavish,
He may the heart of broomstick ravish.
The man whose parts in Taverns shine,
Doates on the merry pipe of wine;
& he who late has got his pate full,
perceives the water pipe is gratefull;
But these are pipes that still are mute,
there is some musick in a flute.
Which since I as a present send,
the presents worth to recommend,
Ile in soft words its praises warble,
translated from Italian marble.
'When ere we hear its strains & closes,
'Enchanted reason sweetly dozes,
'on laps of nymphs, & beds of roses;
'the Soul that all its charms admires,
'for lodgings in the ear enquires;
'Gay pictures do the Fancy store;
'& passions felt but heard no more.
All that my author says is true,

When th' instrument is playd by you.
& least you think I came by this ill,
Splut her was preed her from a whistle.

Love in Disguise

To stifle Passion is no easy Thing,
A Heart in Love is always on the Wing;
The bold Betrayer flutters still,
And fans the Breath prepar'd to tell:
It melts the Tongue, and tunes the Throat,
And moves the Lips to form the Note;
And when the Speech is lost,
It then sends out its Ghost,
A little Sigh,
To say we dye.
'Tis strange the Air that Cools, a Flame shou'd prove,
But wonder not, it is the Air of Love.
Yet Chloris I can make my Love look well,
And cover bleeding Wounds I can't conceal,
My Words such artful Accents break,
You think I rather act than speak:
My Sighs enliven'd thro' a Smile,
Your unsuspecting Thoughts beguile;
My Eyes are vary'd so,
You can't their Wishes know:
And I'm so gay,
You think I play.
Happy Contrivance! such as can't be priz'd,
To Live in Love, and yet to Live disguis'd.

An Eclogue

Now early shepheards ore ye meadow pass,
And print long foot-steps in the glittering grass;
The Cows unfeeding near the cottage stand,
By turns obedient to the Milkers hand,
Or loytring stretch beneath an Oaken shade,
Or lett the suckling Calf defraud the maid.

When Harry softly trod the shaven lawn,
Harry a youth from Citty care with drawn,
Unlike the lowly swains Arcadia bore,
Their Pipes but sounded in the days of yore:
Now Gales regardless range the Vaults above,
And No fond swain believes they sigh for love,
No more the Waters sympathising weep;

Our Lads unskilld in musick tend the sheep;
For Tom and Will our Yellow Ceres waves,
And Kate instead of Chloris binds ye sheaves.
Sicilian Muse thy higher strains explore,
Thy higher strains may suit with nature more.

Long was the pleasing Walk he wanderd through;
A Coverd arbour closd ye distant View:
Cross-sloping railes a lattice front supplyd,
And twind the flowring woodbine crept aside.
There rests the Youth, and while the featherd throng
Raise their wild Musick, thus contrives a song.

Here wafted o're by mild Etesian air
Thou Country Goddess Beautious Health repair;
Here lett my breast thro' quiv'ring trees inhale,
Thy rosy blessings with the Morning gale.
The Months that wake ye fragrant year renew,
The Sun is golden and the skys are blue,
Fair silver sprinklings fill ye walk with light,
The boughs are verdant and the blossoms white;
Yet what are these, or those, or all I see,
Ah Joyless all! if not enjoyd with thee.

Come Country Goddess come, nor thou suffice,
But bring thy Mountain Sister Exercise.
Calld by thy lively voice she turns her pace,
Her winding horn proclaims a finishd chace,
She bounds the rocks, she skims ye level plain,
Dogs hawks and horses croud her early train,
Her hardy face repells the tanning wind,
And lines and meshes loosely float behind.
These all as means of toil the feeble see,
But these are helps of pleasure all wth thee.

O come the Goddess of my rural Song,
And bring thy daughter calm content along,
Dame of the ruddy cheek & laughing eye,
From whose bright presence clouds of trouble fly;
For her I mow my walks, I platt my bowrs,
Clip my low hedges & support my flowrs.
To wellcome her this summer seat I drest;
And here Ile court her when she comes to rest.
She'le lead from exercise to learned Ease,
And Change again, & teach ye change to please.

Joy to my soul! I feel the Goddess nigh,
The face of Nature cheers as well as I.
Ore the flat Green refreshing Breezes run
To make young Dazys blow beneath the sun;
While limpid waters to the bottom seen

Lave the soft margin of the lovely Green,
Brisk chirping birds from all the compass rove
To tempt ye warbling Ecchoes of ye grove,
High sunny summits, deeply-shaded dales,
Thick mossy banks, and flowry winding vales,
With Various prospect gratify the sight,
And scatter fixd attention with delight.
Till the raisd soul by gay confusion wrought
Within a sphear of pleasure rolls on thought.
Here beautious Health for all ye year remain,
When ye next comes I'le charm thee thus again.

But rustling boughs yt round my temples play,
Drive the deep doze of Vision swift away.
Lett sloth ly softning till the noon in down,
Or lolling fan her in the sultry town,
Unnerve with rest & turn her own disease,
Or foster others in luxurious ease.
I mount the Courser, call ye deep'ning hounds,
The fox unkennelld flys to covert grounds.
I lead where stags through cumbrous thickets tread,
And shake the saplings with their branching head.
I make the falcons wing their airy way,
And soar to seize, or stooping, strike ye prey.
To snare ye fish I fix ye luring bait.
To Wound ye fowl I load ye gun with fate.
Tis thus through changing shows of toil I range,
And strength & pleasure rise in ev'ry change.
Here beautious Health for all ye year remain,
When the next comes Ile charm thee thus again.

Now friends my life with usefull talk refine,
And Tullys Tusculum revives in mine.
Now to grave books I bid ye mind retreat,
And such as make me rather good than great.
Or o're the works of easy fancy rove,
Where pipes and innocence amuse ye grove:
The Native Bard that on Sicilian plains
Best sung the lowly manners of the Swains;
Great Maro's Muse, that in the finest light
Paints Country prospects and the charms of sight;
Strong Spencers Calender, whose Moons appear
To trace their Changes in the rural year;
Sweet Pope whose lays along with Nature run
Through all the seasons which divide ye sun;
The tender Philips lines, who lately tryd
To plant Arcadia by the Severn side;
And Gentle Gays that happily explore
Those British Shepheards Spencer sought before.
The Soft Amusements bring content Along,
And Fancy, void of sorrow, runs to song.

Here Beautious Health for all ye year remain,
When the next comes Ile charm thee thus again.

So sung the Youth. But now ye cool wth drew;
The sun had dryd the shaking drops of dew,
Then ragd with flames insufferably bright,
& shot the lattice with a checq'ring light;
The Zephirs fall, tho' not to hear his lay,
And in his shade the Flyes offensive play.

A Dream

Just when ye dead of night began to fail
& boding visions senceless dreams expell
Methought a matron stood beside my bed
Upon her face a wondrous sweetness playd
& pointed Glorys dressd the modest visions head
My tongue grew speechless & my eyes were fixt
By silent fear with admiration mixt
She to my lips a living coal apply's
Perhaps from some well pleasing sacrifice
Then thus she said while I more courage found
To bear her sight & hear ye heav'nly sound
From the bright realms my vot'ries have I came
Saints are my vot'ries Piety my name
Oft do I come but often am dispisd
Happy were all if all my favour prizd
Now my best offers to yr soul I give
Accept these offers O be mine & live
Ile teach you how to pray for wt you want
& when I teach you God yr prayr will grant
Ile teach you your redeemer to rehearse
& glide in flames of love along yr verse
Lett other men describe wth flowing lines
How Damon courts or Amarillis shines
But for your subject chuse a theme divine
Fames their reward while heaven it self is thine
& then since Angells sing of nought below
They'le sing like men but like an angell you
Be thou my bard (& as these words she said
She powrd a sacred unction on my head
Then thus proceeded) Be thy muse thy Zeal
Dare to be good & all my Joys reveal
If Drunkards to their Deity apply
A short contentment & a fleeting Joy
Apply to me true peace & lasting bliss
I should not dress in weaker charms yn his
New-paint ye love yt hov'ring over beds
From purple wings his guilty pleasures sheds

His bow be sable sable be the darts
But tingd with endless flame to scorch our hearts
His bones without the sanguin stream or vital parts
But above all employ thy utmost powr
On love Divine twill need it all & more
Oh boundless Goodness to poor mankind shown
Tell but the fact, lett rhetorick alone,
No colours can become it like its own.
Draw a Descending Jesus from ye sky
Make the great being in a manger ly
Of men despisd of men he came to save
Pursu'd afflicted to ye very grave
Make ye great being cheerfully submitt
& me like Mary weeping at his feet
Much have I said & more woud tell you yet
But raptures smother what I woud repeat
My thoughts grow giddy while I strive to sound
The height & depth of love wthout a bound
My God I cannot comprehend thy wayes
But what I cannot comprehend Ile prayse

& then With raptures in her mouth she fled
The Cloud (for on a cloud she seemd to tread)
Its curles unfolded & around her spread
My downy rest the warmth of fancy broke
& when my thoughts grew settled thus I spoke

Ah Gracious Lord make all my dreams like this
& make mine innocence compose my bliss
When reason lyes Asleep & leaves to reign
May my good Angell my passions restrain
Or I must wake to find upon my breast
The gaudy forms more deep yn ere imprest
They'le make my reason's victorys in vain
& make my former habits mine again
Thus if the snake wch hardly moves the tail
To shun the conqu'ring season takes a cell
If nature in a sleep a skin prepare
give him more strength & make him look more fair
He finds his robe is changd fm what he wore
He proudly shoots along ye sunny shore
& hunts the man fm whom he fled before.

Hesiod or The Rise of Woman

What ancient times (those times we fancy wise)
Have left on long record of woman's rise,
What morals teach it, and what fables hide,
What author wrote it, how that author dy'd

All these I sing. In Greece they fram'd the tale
(In Greece 'twas thought a woman might be frail);
Ye modern beauties! where the Poet drew
His softest pencil, thin he dreamt of you;
And, warn'd by him, ye wanton pens beware
How Heaven's concern'd to vindicate the fair.
The case was Hesiod's; he the fable writ;
Some think with meaning, some with idle wit:
Perhaps 'tis either, as the ladies please;
I wave the contest, and commence the lays.
In days of yore (no matter what or when,
'Twas ere the low creation swarm'd with men)
That one Prometheus, sprung of heavenly birth,
(Our Author's song can witness) liv'd on earth:
He carv'd the turf to mould a manly frame,
And stole from Jove his animating flame.
The sly contrivance o'er Olympus ran,
When thus the Monarch of the Stars began.
O vers'd in arts! whose daring thoughts aspire,
To kindle clay with never-dying fire!
Enjoy thy glory past, that gift was thine;
The next thy creature meets, be fairly mine:
And such a gift, a vengence so design'd,
As suits the counsel of a God to find;
A pleasing bosom-cheat, a specious ill,
Which felt the curse, yet covets still to feel.
He said, and Vulcan straight the Sire commands,
To temper mortar with Etherial hands;
In such a shape to mould a rising fair;
As virgin goddesses are proud to wear;
To make her eyes with diamond-water shine,
And form her organs for a voice divine
'Twas thus the Sire ordain'd; the Power obey'd;
And work'd, and wonder'd at the work he made;
The fairest, softest, sweetest frame beneath,
Now made to seem, now more than seem to breathe.
As Vulcan ends, the cheerful Queen of Charms
Clasp'd the new-panting creature in her arms:
From that embrace a fine complexion spread,
Where mingled whiteness glow'd with softer red.
Then in a kiss she breath'd her various arts,
Of triffling prettily with wounded hearts;
A mind for love, but still a changing mind;
The lisp affected, and the glance design'd
The sweet confusing blush, the secret wink,
The gentle swimming walk, the courteous sink;
The stare for strangeness fit, for scorn the frown;
For decent yielding, looks declining down;
The practis'd languish, where well-feign'd desire
Would its own melting in a mutual fire;
Gay smiles to comfort; April showers to move;

And all the nature, all the art of love.
Gold scepter'd Juno next exalts the fair;
Her touch endows her with imperious air,
Self-valuing fancy, highly-crested pride,
Strong soverign will, and some desire to chide;
For which an eloquence, that aims to vex,
With native tropes of anger, arms the sex.
Minerva, skillful goddess, train'd the maid
To twirle the spindle by the twisting thread;
To fix the loom, instruct the reeds to part,
Cross the long weft, and close the web with art,
A useful gift; but what profuse expense,
What world of fashions, took its rise from hence!
Young Hermes next, a close contriving god,
Her brows encircled with his serpent rod;
Then plots and fair excuses fill'd her brain,
The views of breaking amorous vows for gain;
The price of favours; the designing arts
That aim at riches in contempt of hearts;
And, for a comfort in the marriage life,
The little pilfering temper of a wife.
Full on the fair his beams Apollo flung,
And fond persuasion tipp'd her easy tongue;
He gave her words, where oily flattery lays
The pleasing colours of the art of praise;,
And wit, to scandal exquisitely prone
Which frets another's spleen to cure its own.
Those sacred Virgins1 whom the bards revere
Tun'd all her voice, and shed a sweetness there,
To make her sense with double charms abound,
Or make her lively nonsense please by sound.
To dress the maid, the decent Graces brought
A robe in all the dies of beauty wrought,
And plac'd their boxes o'er a rich brocade,
Where pictured Loves on every cover play'd;
Then spread those implements that Vulcan's art
Had frame'd to merit Cytherea's heart;
The wire to curl, the close indented comb
To call the locks, that lightly wander, home;
And chief, the mirror,where the ravish'd maid
Beholds and loves her own reflected shade.
Fair Flora lent her stores; the purpled Hours
Confin'd her tresses with a wreath of flowers;
Within the wreath arose a radiant crown;
A veil pellucid hung depending down;
Back roll'd her azure veil with surpent fold,
The pursled border deck'd the floor with gold.
Her robe (which closely by the girdle brac'd
Reveal'd the beauties of a slender waist)
Flow'd to the feet, to copy Venus' air,
When Venus' statues have a robe to wear.

The new-sprung creature, finish'd thus for harms,
Adjusts her habit, practices her charms,
With blushes glows, or shines with lively smiles,
Confirms her will, or recollects her wiles:
Then, conscious of her worth, with easy pace
Glides by the glass, and turning views her face.
A finer flax than what they wrought before,
Through Time's deep cave, the Sister Fates explore,
Then fix the loom, their fingers nimbly weave,
And thus their toil prophetic songs deceive.
Flow from the rock, my flax! and swiftly flow,
Pursue thy thread; the spindle runs below.
A creature fond and changing, fair and vain,
The creature woman, rises now to reign.
New beauty blooms, a beauty form'd to fly;
New love begins, a love produc'd to die;
New parts distress the troubled scenes of life,
The fondling mistress, and the ruling wife.
"Men born to labour, all with pains provide;
Women have time to sacrifice to pride:
They want the care of man, their want they know,
And dress to please with heart-alluring show;
The show prevailing, for the sway contend,
And make a servant where they meet a friend.
Thus in a thousand wax-erected forts
A loitering race the painful bee supports;
From sun to sun, from bank to bank he flies,
With honey loads his bag, with wax his thighs;
Fly where he will, at home the race remain,
Prune the silk dress, and murmuring eat the gain.
Yet here and there we grant a gentle bride,
Whose temper betters by the father's side;
Unlike the rest that double human care,
Fond to relieve, or resolute to share:
Happy the man whom thus his stars advance!
The curse is general, but the blessing chance.
Thus sung the Sisters, while the Gods admire
Their beauteous creature, made for man in ire;
The young Pandora she, whom all contend
To make too perfect not to gain her end:
Then bid the winds, that fly to breathe the spring
Return to bear her on a gentle wing;
With wafting airs the winds obsequious blow,
And land the shining vengeance safe below.
A golden coffer in her hand she bore,
The present treacherous, but the bearer more;
'Twas fraught with pangs; for Jove ordain'd above
That gold should aid, and pangs attend on love.
Her gay descent the man perceiv'd afar,
Wondering he ran to catch the falling star:
But so surpris'd, as none but he can tell,

Who lov'd so quickly, and who lov'd so well.
O'er all his veins the wandering passion burns,
He calls her Nymph, and every Nymph by turns.
Her form to lovely Venus he prefers;
Or swears that Venus' must be such as hers.
She, proud to rule, yet strangely fram'd to teaze,
Neglects his offers while her airs she plays,
Shoots scornful glances from the bended frown,
In brisk disorder trips it up and down;
Then hums a careless tune to lay the storm,
And sits, and blushes, smiles, and yields in form.
"Now take what Jove design'd," she softly cry'd,
"This box they portion, and myself the bride."
Fir'd with the prospect of the double charms,
He snatch'd the box, and bride, with eager arms.
Unhappy man! to whom so bright she shone,
The fatal gift, her tempting self, unknown!
The winds were silent, all the waves asleep,
And heaven was trac'd upon the flattering deep:
But, whilst he looks unmindful of a storm,
And thinks the water wears a stable form,
What dreadful din around his ears shall rise!
What frowns confuse his picture of the skies!
At first the creature man was fram'd alone,
Lord of himself, and all the world his own.
For him the Nymphs in green forsook the woods,
For him the Nymphs in blue forsook the floods;
In vain the Satyrs rage, the Tritons rave,
They bore him heroes in the secret cave.
No care destroy'd, no sick disorder prey'd,
No bending age his sprightly form decay'd,
No wars were known, no females heard to rage,
And, Poets tell us, 'twas a golden age.
When woman came, those ills the box confin'd
Burst furious out, and poison'd all the wind,
From point to point, from pole to pole they flew,
Spread as they went, and in the progress grew:
the Nymphs regretting left the mortal race,
And altering nature wore a sickly face:
New terms of folly rose, new states of care;
New plagues to suffer, and to please, the Fair!
The days of whining, and of wild intrigues,
Commenc'd, or finish'd with the breach of leagues;
The mean designs of well-dissembled love;
The sordid matches never join'd above:
Abroad the labour, and at home the noise,
(Man's double sufferings for domestic joys)
The curse of jealousy; expense and strife;
Divorce, the public brand of shameful life;
The rival's sword; the qualm that takes the fair;
Disdain for passion, passion in despair

These, and a thousand yet unnam'd, we find;
Ah fear the thousand yet unnam'd behind!
Thus on Parnassus tuneful Hesiod sung,
The mountains echoed, and the valley rung,
The sacred goves a fix'd attention show,
The crystal Helicon forebore to flow,
The sky grew bright, and (if his verse be true)
The Muses came to give the laurel too.
But what avail'd the verdant prize of wit,
If Love swore vengeance for the tales he writ?
Ye Fair offended, hear your friend relate
What heavy judgment prov'd the writer's fate,
Though when it happen'd no relation clears,
'Tis thought in five, or five and twenty years.
Where, dark and silent, with a twisted shade
the neighbouring woods a native arbour made,
There oft a tender pair, for amorous play
Returing, toy'd the ravish'd hours away;
A Locrian youth, the gentle Troilus he,
A fair Milesian, kind Evanthe she:
But swelling nature in a fatal hour
Betray'd the secrets of the conscious bower;
The dire disgrace her brothers count their own,
And track her steps to make its author known.
It chanc'd one evening, 'twas the lover's day,
Conceal'd in brakes the jealous kindred lay;
When Hesiod, wandering, mus'd along the plain,
And fix'd his seat where love had fix'd the scene;
A strong suspicion straight possess their mind,
(For Poets ever were a gentle kind)
But when Evanthe near the passage stood,
Flung back a doubtful look, and shot the wood,
"Now take (at once they cry) thy due reward,"
And, urg'd with erring rage, assault the Bard.
His corpse the sea receiv'd. The dolphins bore
('Twas all the gods would do) the corpse to shore.
Methinks I view the dead with pitying eyes
And see the dreams of ancient wisdom rise;
I see the Muses round the body cry,
But hear a Cupid loudly laughing by;
He wheels his arrow with insulting hand,
And thus inscribes the moral on the sand.
"Here Hesiod lies: ye future Bards, beware
How far your moral tales incense the Fair.
Unlov'd, unloving, 'twas his fate to bleed;
Without his quiver, Cupid caus'd the deed:
He judg'd this turn of malice justly due,
And Hesiod dy'd for joys he never knew."

To A Young Lady, On Her Translation Of The Story Of Phoebus And Daphne, From Ovid

In Phœbus Wit (as Ovid said)
Enchanting Beauty woo'd;
In Daphne Beauty coily fled,
While vainly Wit pursu'd.
But when you trace what Ovid writ,
A diff'rent Turn we view;
Beauty no longer flies from Wit,
Since both are joyn'd in You.
Your Lines the wondrous Change impart,
From whence our Lawrels spring;
In Numbers fram'd to please the Heart,
And merit what they Sing.
Methinks thy Poet's gentle Shade
Its Wreath presents to Thee;
What Daphne owes you as a Maid,
She pays you as a Tree.

On Embroydring

How justly art when Cælia aids so well
Contends her ms nature to excell
The slender needles in that hand create
Such forms as hers but of a better date
The silk is placd the winding traces laid
& the gay scene with rising figures spread
here springing lillies opening roses dress
In such sweet colours & so fixd a grace
They outdoe all but those wthin her face
The well turnd leaves if by the natrall shown
You'd think they both were workd or both had grown
So strange yet beautious birds are here designd
As if she had increasd the Phœnix kind
Sure had she livd wn poets tho below
Where meritt pleaded cou'd a heavn bestow
The wondrows product of her needle here
Had made her self a goddess it a starr.

Oh may no moth so rare a piece approach
May nought corrupt it with unhallowd touch
May nothing—but alas I wast my prayr
My wishes rise to loose themselves in air.
This work wch angells wou'd not blush to own
Must once the common road of ruin run
then quickly fairest on yr life reflect
Nor all your downy hours of youth neglect
Think you behold this lovely piece decayd
Think you are brighter yet must sooner fade

Then quitt your folly be no more severe
Why woud you have no difference appear
In how the ugly live & how the fair
& tell me Celie where the diffrence lyes
'Twixt those who Cant & those who wont possess
When both alike are distanc't fm their bliss.

Psalm 67

Have mercy mercy Lord on us
& grant thy blessed grace
Direct us in ye way of life
By th' sunshine of thy face
So all the nations on the earth
Shall praise my god & king
& when they see thy saving health
Shall in a chorus sing.
Let all thy people praise thy name
& lift their voice on high
Let ym extoll it so with shouts
That heav'n may ring with Joy
Rejoyce o earth thy gods thy Judge
Be glad who righteous are
He'le rule ye world with equity
& govern it with fear
Let all thy people praise thy name
& lift their voice on high
Let thm extoll it so with shouts
that heav'n may ring with Joy
Then god shall open heavens gates
& pour down all his store
He shall you bless with great encrease
& you shall him adore.

On the Death of Mr Viner

Is Viner Dead? and shall each Muse become
Silent as Death, and as his Musick Dumb?
Shall he depart without a poet's Praise,
Who oft to Harmony has tun'd their Lays?
Shall he, who knew the Elegance of Sound,
Find no one voice to sing him to the Ground?
musick and poetry are Sister-Arts,
Shew a like Genius, and consenting Hearts:
My Soul with his is secretly ally'd,
And I am forc'd to speak, since viner dy'd.
Oh that my Muse, as once his Notes, could swell!

That I might all his Praises fully tell;
That I might say with how much skill he play'd,
How nimbly four extended Strings survey'd;
How Bow and Fingers, with a noble Strife,
Did raise the vocal fiddle into Life;
How various Sounds, in various Order rang'd,
By unobserv'd Degrees minutely chang'd;
Thro' a vast Space could in Divisions run,
Be all distinct, yet all agree in One:
And how the fleeter Notes could swiftly pass,
And skip alternately from Place to Place;
The Strings could with a sudden Impulse bound,
Speak every Touch, and tremble into Sound.

The liquid Harmony, a tuneful Tide,
Now seem'd to rage, anon wou'd gently glide;
By Turns would ebb and flow, would rise and fall,
Be loudly daring, or be softly small:
While all was blended in one common Name,
Wave push'd on Wave, and all compos'd a Stream.

The diff'rent tones melodiously combin'd,
Temper'd with Art, in sweet Confusion join'd;
The Soft, the Strong, the Clear, the Shrill, the Deep,
Would sometimes soar aloft, and sometimes creep;
While ev'ry Soul upon his Motions hung,
As tho' it were in tuneful Concert strung.
His Touch did strike the Fibres of the Heart,
And a like Trembling secretly impart;
Where various Passions did by Turns succeed,
He made it chearful, and he made it bleed;
Could wind it up into a glowing Fire,
Then shift the Scene, and teach it to expire.

Oft have I seen him on a Publick Stage,
Alone the gaping Multitude engage;
The Eyes and Ears of each Spectator draw,
Command their Thoughts, and give their Passions Law;
While other Musick in Oblivion drown'd,
Seem'd a dead Pulse, or a neglected Sound.

Alas! he's gone, our Great Apollo's dead,
And all that's sweet and tuneful with him fled.
hibernia—with one universal Cry,
Laments its Loss, and speaks his elegy.
Farewel, thou Author of refin'd Delight,
Too little known, too soon remov'd from Sight;
Those Fingers, which such Pleasure did convey,
Must now become to stupid Worms a prey:
Thy grateful fiddle with for ever stand
A silent Mourner for its master's Hand:

Thy art is only to be match'd Above,
Where Musick reigns, and in that Musick Love:
Where Thou wilt with the happy chorus join,
And quickly Thy melodious soul refine
To the exalted pitch of Harmony Divine.

Oft Have I Read That Innocence Retreats

Oft have I read that Innocence retreats
Where cooling streams salute ye summer Seats
Singing at ease she roves ye field of flowrs
Or safe with shepheards lys among the bowrs
But late alas I crossd a country fare
And found No Strephon nor Dorinda there
There Hodge & William Joynd to cully ned
While Ned was drinking Hodge & William dead
There Cicely Jeard by day the slips of Nell
& ere ye night was ended Cicely fell
Are these the Virtues which adorn the plain
Ye bards forsake your old Arcadian Vein
To sheep those tender Innocents resign
The place where swains & nymphs are said to shine
Swains twice as Wicked Nymphs but half as sage
Tis sheep alone retrieve ye golden age.

Bacchus or, The Vines Of Lesbos

As Bacchus ranging at his leisure,
(Io Bacchus! king of pleasure)
Charm'd the wide world with drink and dances,
And all his thousand airy fancies;
Alas! he quite forgot the while
His fav'rite vines in Lesbos isle.

The God returning ere they died,
Ah! see my jolly Fawns, he cried,
The leaves but hardly born are red,
And the bare arms for pity spread;
The beasts afford a rich manure,
Fly, my boys, and bring the cure,
Up the mountains, down the vales;
Thro' the woods, and o'er the dales;
For this, if full the clusters grow,
Your bowls shall doubly overflow.

So chear'd, with more officious haste
They bring the dung of ev'ry beast,

The loads they wheel, the roots they bare,
They lay the rich manure with care,
While oft he calls to labour hard,
And names as oft the red reward.

The plants revive, new leaves appear,
The thick'ning clusters load the year;
The season swiftly purple grew,
The grapes hung dangling deep with blue.

A vineyard ripe a day serene
Now calls them all to work again;
The Fawns thro' ev'ry furrow shoot
To load their flaskets with the fruit;
And now the vintage early trod,
The wines invite the jovial God.

Strow the roses, raise the song,
See the master comes along!
Lusty Revel join'd with Laughter,
Whim and Frolic follow after.
The Fawns beside the vatts remain
To shew the work, and reap the gain.

All around, and all around
They sit to riot on the ground,
A vessel stands amidst the ring,
And here they laugh, and there they sing;
Or rise a jolly jolly band,
And dance about it hand in hand;
Dance about, and shout amain,
Then sit to laugh and sing again.

But, as an antient author sung,
The vine manur'd with ev'ry dung,
From ev'ry creature strangely drew,
A tang of brutal nature too;
'Twas hence in drinking on the lawns
New turns of humour seiz'd the Fawns.

Here one was crying out, by Jove!
Another, fight me in the grove;
This wounds a friend, and that the trees;
The Lion's temper reign'd in these.

Another grins and leaps about,
And keeps a merry world of rout,
And talks impertinently free;
And twenty talk the same as he:
Chatt'ring, airy, idle, kind:
These take the Monkey-turn of mind.

Here one who saw the nymphs that stood
To peep upon them from the wood,
Steals off, to try if any maid
Be lagging late beneath the shade;
While loose discourse another raises
In naked Nature's plainest phrases;
And ev'ry glass he drinks enjoys
With change of nonsense, lust and noise;
Mad and careless, hot and vain,
Such as these the Goat retain.

Another drinks and casts it up,
And drinks and wants another cup,
Solemn, silent, and sedate,
Ever long and ever late,
Full of meats and full of wine;
This takes his temper from the swine.

Here some who hardly seem to breathe,
Drink and hang the jaw beneath,
Gaping, tender, apt to weep;
Their natures alter'd by the sheep.

'Twas thus one autumn all the crew
(If what the Poets sing be true)
While Bacchus made the merry feast
Inclin'd to one or other beast;
And since 'tis said for many a mile
He spread the vines of Lesbos isle.

On The Castle Of Dublin, Anno 1715

This House and Inhabitants both well agree,
And resemble each other as near can be;
One half is decay'd, and in want of a Prop,
The other new built, but not finish'd a-top.

On Ye Queens Death

The Persians us'd at setting of ye sunn
To howl, as if he nere again should runn
They onely acted it but we indeed
Must doot for all that lovely was is fled
All that was great good Just & vertuous Dead.
The poets of ye graces do relate
That they did upon none but Venus wait

'Tis false or this was she for in each eye
Of hers ten thousand graces you might spy
So many her vertues were Death heard ym told
Mistook ye for her dayes & thought her old
Yet she is gone all that was lovely fled,
All that was great good Just & vertuous dead
When Romulus was taken to ye gods
& Ceesar mounted to ye blest abodes
In floods & earth-quakes nature Largely grievd
For these her Heroes heaven had receivd
She wept indeed then now she cannot weep
The stillness of ye waves but shows ye deep
The greatness of ye Loss putts all her faculties asleep.

The Horse & Olive or Warr & Peace

With Moral tale let Ancient wisdome move
Which thus I sing to make ye moderns wise
Strong Neptune once with sage Minerva strove
And rising Athens was the Victors prize
By Neptune Plutus guardian Powr of gain
By great Minerva Bright Apollo stood
But Jove superiour Bad ye side obtain
Which best contrivd to do ye nation good
Then Neptune striking from the parted ground
The Warlike horse came pawing on ye plain
And as it tossd its main & prancd around
By this he crys Ile make the people reign
The Goddess smiling gently bowd ye spear
And rather thus they shall be blessd she said
Then upwards shooting in ye Vernal air
With loaded boughs ye fruitfull Olive spread
Jove saw what gifts ye rival Powrs designd
Then took th' impartial scales resolvd to show
If greater bliss in warlike pomp we find
Or in ye calm which peacefull times bestow
On Neptunes part he placd victorious days
Gay trophys won & fame extending wide
But plenty safety science arts & ease
Minerva's scale with greater weight supplyd
Fierce warr devours whom gentle Peace woud save
Sweet peace restores wt angry warr destroys
Warr made for peace with that rewards ye brave
While Peace its pleasures from it self enjoys
Hence Vanquishd Neptune to ye Sea withdrew
Hence Wise Minerva ruld Athenian lands
Her Athens hence in arts & honour grew
And still her Olives deck pacifick hands
From fables thus disclosd a Monarchs mind

May form Just rules to chuse ye truly great
And subjects wearyd with distresses find
Whose kind endeavours most befriend a state
Evn Britain here may learn to place her love
If Citys won her kingdomes wealth have cost
If Anna's thoughts ye Patriot soules approve
Whose cares restore yt wealth ye wars had lost
But if we ask ye Moral to disclose
Whom best Europa's patroness it calls
Great Anna's title no exception knows
And unapplyd in this ye fable falls
With her no Neptune or Minerva vyes
When ere she pleasd her troops to conquest flew
When ere she pleases peaceful times arise
She gave the horse & gives ye Olive too.

Song II

When thy Beauty appears
In its Graces and Airs,
All bright as an Angel new dropt from the Sky;
At distance I gaze, and am aw'd by my Fears,
So strangely you dazzle my Eye!
But when without Art,
Your kind Thoughts you impart,
When your Love runs in Blushes thro' ev'ry Vein;
When it darts from your Eyes, when it pants in your Heart,
Then I know you're a Woman again.
There's a Passion and Pride
In our Sex, (she reply'd,)
And thus (might I gratify both) I wou'd do:
Still an Angel appear to each Lover beside,
But still be a Woman to you.

Psalm 113

Ye who ye Ld of host adore
O praise his name alone
O send his praises to ye skyes
Untill they reach his throne
His throne who's ever ever blest
Whose great whose holy name
Still great still holy will endure
Who ever is ye same
Morning & night letts praise yt god
Who gave us morn & night.
Above all thinges yt are he is

Above ye heav'ns his might
tell of his mercy humbleness
Yt tho so high he be
Yet he will stoop to mind such poor
Such wretched things as we
Tell of his Justice too yt from
A mean & lowly state
Ye poor & innocent he does
Among ev'n princes sett
Those who with barreness were curst
He blesses wth increase,
That happy thus in all they wish
They might his goodness praise.

Psalm 116

Ime Pleasd that Heaven hears my cry,
Regards me when I pray,
Ime pleasd, & in a gratefull Joy,
Will worship every day.
God heard my voice, & I escapd,
Tho death had spread his snare,
Tho hell with horrid pleasure gapd
To be my sepulchre.
& when with troubles Ime besett
Again Ile call on thee,
Ah help the wretch that cry's for aid,
My God deliver me.
How Just how gratious is the Lord,
How mercyfull is he?
He to the simple help affords,
Yes, he has succourd me.
Then rest my soul secure from fear,
Since he so kind has been,
Since he has kept my eyes from tears,
My sliding feet from sin.
Tis he who keeps me living still,
& when sore vext I cryd;
Since mankind is as weak as ill,
In him I must confide.
How shall I then the God reward
Who did my all bestow?
To pray, & thank, & praise thee Lord,
Is all that I can do.
In publick will I pay my vows,
& tell thy mercy's ore,
Tell how our lives are precious
To thee, whom we adore.
Behold me Lord, for I am thine,

My parents so have been;
Behold me Lord, for thou art mine,
By thee I'me freed from sin.
Then all shall hear my ready tongue,
Extoll thy name on high,
That all by my example won,
May praise as well as I.

Epigram

The greatest Gifts that Nature does bestow,
Can't unassisted to Perfection grow:
A scanty Fortune clips the Wings of Fame,
And checks the Progress of a rising Name;
Each dastard Vertue drags a Captive's Chain,
And moves but slowly, for it moves with Pain.
Domestick Cares sit hard upon the Mind,
And cramp those Thoughts which shou'd be unconfin'd;
The Cries of Poverty alarm the Soul,
Abate its Vigour, its Designs controul:
The Stings of Want inflict the Wounds of Death,
And Motion always ceases with the Breath.
The Love of Friends is found a languid Fire,
That glares but faintly, and will soon expire;
Weak is its Force, nor can its Warmth be great,
A feeble Light begets a feeble Heat.
Wealth is the Fuel that must feed the Flame,
It dyes in Rags, and scarce deserves a Name.

On A Ladys Lace Shown For A Favour

As Nelly to a chamber got
To take her leave of Ned
She loosd her lace & Cast a knot
(Ah why unlacd the maid.).
Now pull the further end she cryd
The Youth obeyd commands
And still the knot ye faster tyd
The more they parted hands
This fancy by the lover seen
She gave the silken braid
And with a kiss or two between
The parting posy said
When this you see remember me
And love me more & more
This knot when you at distance drew
Came closer than before.

Holy Jesus! God of Love!
Look with pity from above,
Shed the precious purple tide
From thine hands, thy feet, thy side,
Let thy streams of comfort roll,
Let them please and fill my soul.
Let me thus for ever be
Full of gladness, full of thee,
This for which my wishes pine
Is the cup of love divine,
Sweet affections flow from hence,
Sweet above the joys of sense;
Blessed Philtre! how we find
Its sacred worships, how the mind
Of all the world forgetful grown,
Can despise an earthly throne,
Raise its thoughts to Realms above,
Think of God, and sing of love.

Love Celestial, wond'rous heat
O beyond expression great!
What resistless charms were thine
In thy good thy best design!
When God was hated, Sin obey'd,
And man undone without thy aid.
From the seats of endless peace
They brought the son, the Lord of grace,
They taught him to receive a birth,
To cloath in flesh, to live on earth,
And after lifted him on high,
And taught him on the Cross to die.

Love Celestial ardent fire,
O extreme of sweet desire!
Spread thy brightly raging flame
Thro' and over all my frame;
Let it warm me let it burn,
Let my corps to ashes turn,
And might thy flame thus act with me
To set the soul from body free,
I next wou'd use thy wings and fly
To meet my Jesus in the sky.

On Content

Grant heav'n that I may chuse my bliss
If you design me worldly Happiness
Tis not Honour thats but air
Glory has but fancied light
Fame as oft speak's false as right
Riches have wings & ever dwell with care
Give me an undistemperd mind
As ye third region undisturbd by wind
Content from passions ever free
To rule ones selfs indeed a monarchy
This I request of thee

Tho all we see are fortunes apes
& change as oft as she their shapes
Tho my kinder fortune leave me
Tho my dearest friends deceive me
I in this universall tide
Firm on heav'ns mercy would abide
& 'mongst ye giddy waves securely ride
Tho they should die
Who never did my love abuse
Perhaps in tears I would my passion vent
But straight again I'de be content
Remembring 'twas th' almighty's deed tho I
should my best relations loose
Ide sighing cry Heav'ns will be done
It did but lend them now it has its own.
Fortune should never be
Adored as a deity by me
She onely makes them fooles who make her great
But still content on earth intent on heav'n I'de be
An equall temper keep in ev'ry state
Nor Care nor fear my destiny
Death when most dreadfull should not fright
Wn ere he comes Ide patiently submitt
Content thus in my soul should build its halcyons nest
As did thy spirit on ye waters rest
& keep an everlasting calm with in my breast.

As Celia With Her Sparrow Playd

As Celia with her Sparrow playd
She took a glass unseen
Her mouth she filld
& while he billd
She spirts ye liquor in
Usd to such sweet such rosy lips
He feard no treach'ry there

But love & such
Were too too much
For one poor bird to bear
Against ye Pretty fluttring fool
The Mighty foes combine
So down he Sunk
Bewitchd or drunk
By Beauty or wth wine
But ere left ye Chirping cup
& dropp'd the little head,
The folks who guess
What Birds express
Have told me thus he said,
How use the various scenes of joy
At various times to reign?
Men kiss'd in one
They drunk anon
Then after kiss'd again.
But Celia shews short life to grasp
A double store of blisses,
While by her Means
A Bird obtains
At once both Drink & kisses.

The Penitent Sinner

Ah that my eyes were fountaines & could poar
Eternall streams from inexhausted stores
Enough but ah enough there cannot be
To drown th' innumerable ills are done by me
Not all my breath t attone ym would suffice
Tho' all were turnd to penitentiall sighs
Ive sinnd my heart & tongue are vain
Ive sinnd my eyes to vice too pronely rove
Slowly to good my limbs to ill they promptly move
Ive sinnd & all my soul's but one continu'd stain
My crimes beyond all number like my hairs are grown
I sink beneath the weight they press they bend me down
Wt Charming looks did ill in acting wear
How lovely ruin did appear
Now but ah I fear too late
Conscience unmasques the guilded cheat
Stript of their borrowd rays the horrid forms I see
& ye gross daub no more deludes my eye
I see I know my wickedness & misery
Fancys too exquisite & nicely paints
My horrid & deserved punishments
No comfortable glympse my eye or thought presents
All all things speak dispair to poor unhappy me

But stay what heavn'ly light
Breakes thro' this black Egyptian night
It strikes my heartstrings wth unusuall bliss
& tunes ym to delight & happiness
It tells me hope remains
& gives me hope to sooth my raging pains
Wthin my breast it plays I feel the sacred flame
I know it tis my saviours name
His suffrings onely can my troubles calm
His blood alones my balm
In him alone I must confide
In him alone who for me di'd
In him who kindly does on sinners call
Who kindly does receive & welcome all
Come come to me his sacred voice has said
Repent ye of your sinns & come to me he cryes
Tho' nere so great & nere so bad
Ile ease you of your load & calm your miseries
Come take my yoak upon you & my burthens bear
Easy my yoak & light my burthens are
Nor need you a hard master fear
Since he who is my servant is my son
A son & servant is wth me all one

Yes I will come my god to thee
I know thou wilt not turn me back
Thou'lt not refuse the offering I make
Altho' so bad so late so mean a one it be
No flood can drown my sinn but one of tears
No arms can conquer sinn but prayers
Behold in tears & pray'rs & sighs I turn
See how unfeignedly I mourn
See in wt pain what grief of soul I ly
Have mercy mercy lord & hear my cry
Oh save me from this deluge of iniquity
Save me my god oh rid me from my fear
Oh save me from dispair
Look on a wounded & repenting heart
Oh ease it of its smart

Wn to my soul thou'st spoken peace
When from its bonds thou wilt my soul release
All my mourning then shall cease
Then all my sorrow shall be turnd to Joy
& then thy mercyes onely shall my soul employ
Oh hear my god my saviour hear
& lett thy goodness towr'ds me soon appear
Arm me wth heavn'ly temperd arms my Lord
Give for my buckler faith & for a sword thy word
Girt up my loins wth truth & on my breast

Lett righteousness be plac't
Thus thus I safely shall oppose
& safely triumph o're my foes
Thus shall I break the force of hell & flee
With a glad heart to thee
To thee who (all my dangers past)
Wilt give thy self to me thy self & heav'n at last
Theres the continuall treasury of bliss
The magazine of happiness
Pleasure there does never Cease
& in æternall Joy I shall remain
Where in æternall glory thou doest reign.

Health, An Eclogue

Now early Shepherds o'er the Meadow pass,
And print long Foot-steps in the glittering Grass;
The Cows neglectful of their Pasture stand,
By turns obsequious to the Milker's Hand.

When Damon softly trod the shaven Lawn,
Damon a Youth from City Cares withdrawn;
Long was the pleasing Walk he wander'd thro',
A cover'd Arbour clos'd the distant view;
There rests the Youth, and while the feather'd Throng
Raise their wild Musick, thus contrives a Song.

Here wafted o'er by mild Etesian Air,
Thou Country Goddess, beauteous Health! repair;
Here let my Breast thro' quiv'ring Trees inhale
Thy rosy Blessings with the Morning Gale.
What are the Fields, or Flow'rs, or all I see?
Ah! tastless all, if not enjoy'd with thee.

Joy to my Soul! I feel the Goddess nigh,
The Face of Nature cheers as well as I;
O'er the flat Green refreshing Breezes run,
The smiling Dazies blow beneath the Sun,
The Brooks run purling down with silver Waves,
The planted Lanes rejoice with dancing Leaves,
The chirping Birds from all the Compass rove
To tempt the tuneful Echoes of the Grove:
High sunny Summits, deeply shaded Dales,
Thick Mossy Banks, and flow'ry winding Vales,
With various Prospect gratify the Sight,
And scatter fix'd Attention in Delight.

Come, Country Goddess, come, nor thou suffice,
But bring thy Mountain-Sister, Exercise.

Call'd by thy lively Voice, she turns her Pace,
Her winding Horn proclaims the finish'd Chace;
She mounts the Rocks, she skims the level Plain,
Dogs, Hawks, and Horses, crowd her early Train;
Her hardy Face repels the tanning Wind,
And Lines and Meshes loosely float behind.
All these as Means of Toil the Feeble see,
But these are helps to Pleasure join'd with thee.

Let Sloth lye softning 'till high Noon in Down,
Or lolling fan her in the sult'ry Town,
Unnerv'd with Rest; and turn her own Disease,
Or foster others in luxurious Ease:
I mount the Courser, call the deep mouth'd Hounds,
The Fox unkennell'd flies to covert Grounds;
I lead where Stags thro' tangled Thickets tread,
And shake the Saplings with their branching Head;
I make the Faulcons wing their airy Way,
And soar to seize, or stooping strike their Prey;
To snare the Fish I fix the luring Bait;
To wound the Fowl I load the Gun with Fate.
'Tis thus thro' change of Exercise I range,
And Strength and Pleasure rise from ev'ry Change.
Here beautious Health for all the Year remain,
When the next comes, I'll charm thee thus again.

Oh come, thou Goddess of my rural Song,
And bring thy Daughter, calm Content, along,
Dame of the ruddy Cheek and laughing Eye,
From whose bright Presence Clouds of Sorrow fly:
For her I mow my Walks, I platt my Bow'rs,
Clip my low Hedges, and support my Flow'rs;
To welcome her, this Summer Seat I drest,
And here I court her when she comes to Rest;
When she from Exercise to learned Ease
Shall change again, and teach the Change to please.

Now Friends conversing my soft Hours refine,
And Tully's Tusculum revives in mine:
Now to grave Books I bid the Mind retreat,
And such as make me rather Good than Great.
Or o'er the Works of easy Fancy rove,
Where Flutes and Innocence amuse the Grove:
The native Bard that on Sicilian Plains
First sung the lowly Manners of the Swains;
Or Maro's Muse, that in the fairest Light
Paints rural Prospects and the Charms of Sight;
These soft Amusements bring Content along,
And Fancy, void of Sorrow, turns to Song.
Here beauteous Health for all the Year remain,
When the next comes, I'll charm thee thus again.

From Realms of never-interrupted peace,
From thy fair station near the throne of Grace,
From Quires of Angells, Joys in endless round,
& endless Harmonys enchanting sound,
Charmd with a zeal the Makers praise to show,
Bright Gift of Verse descend, & here below
My ravishd heart with raisd affection fill,
& warbling ore the Soul incline my will.
Among thy pomp lett rich expression wait,
Lett ranging numbers form thy train compleat,
While at thy motions thro' the ravishd sky
Sweet Sounds & Eccho's sweet-resounding fly,
& where thy feet with gliding beauty tread
Lett Fancys flowry spring erect its head.

It comes it comes with unaccustomd light,
The tracts of airy Thought grow wondrous bright,
Its notions ancient Memory reviews,
& Young Invention new design pursues,
To some attempt my will & wishes press,
& pleasure raisd in hope forebodes success.

My God from whom proceed the Gifts divine
My God the gift I think I feel is thine.
Be this no vain Illusion which I find,
Nor natures Impulse on the passive mind,
But reasons act, producd by good desire,
By Grace enlivend with celestiall fire:
While base Conceits like misty sons of night
Before such beams of Glory wing their flight;
& frail Affections born of earth decay
Like weeds that wither in the warmer ray.

I thank thee Father with a gratefull mind,
Man's undeserving & thy mercy kind.
I now perceive I long to sing thy praise,
I now perceive I long to find my lays
The Sweet incentives of anothers love,
& sure such Longings have their rise above.
My resolution stands confirmed within,
My Lines aspiring eagerly begin.
Begin my lines to such a subject due
That aids our Labours & rewards ym too;
Begin while Canaan opens to mine eyes,
Where Soules & Songs divinely formd arise.

As one, whom ore ye Sweetly varyd meads
Intire Recess or Lonely Pleasure leads
To verdurd banks, to paths adornd with flowrs,
To shady trees, to closely-weaving bowrs,
To bubbling fountains, & aside ye stream
That softly gliding soothes a waking dream,
Or bears ye thought inspird with heat along,
& with fair images improves a song.
Through sacred Anthems so may Fancy range
So still from beauty still to beauty change
So feel delights in all the radiant way,
& with sweet numbers what it feeles repay.
For this I call that Ancient Time appear
& bring his rolls to serve in method here,
His rolls which acts that endless honour claim,
Have rankd in order for ye voice of Fame.
My call is favourd, Time fm first to last
Unwinds his years, the Present sees ye Past,
I view their circles as he turns ym o're,
& fix my footsteps where he went before.

The Page unfolding woud atop disclose
Where sounds melodious in their birth arose;
Where first the Morning starrs together sung;
Where first their harps the Sons of Glory strung
With Shouts of Joy, while Halelujahs rise
To prove the Chorus of Eternall skys.
Rich sparkling strokes the letters Doubly gild,
& all's with Love & admiration filld.

Now Kind Now Coy Wth How Much Change

Now kind now coy wth how much change
You feed my fierce desire
As if to more extravagance
Youd manage up the fire
In vain if this your meaning be
In vain you use these wayes
Tis æqually as hard for me
To love you more as less
To other nymphs bequeath yr arts
Whose eyes more faintly shine
Or practise them at least on hearts
Which love you not like mine.

Out Of Greek

The things that Mortals love are mortal too
& swiftly transient fleet before the view
Or if with man a longer while they stay
Man swiftly transient fleets himself away.

When Haizy Clouds Obscure The Night

When Haizy clouds obscure the night
No more the starrs afford us light
When ruffling winds arise at sea
Tho smooth as glass & clear as day
The mudd workes up the ocean frys
& thickend waters stopp the eyes,
The brook which from the mountain flows
Oft runs astray if rocks oppose
Then woud you with the piercing sight
Of reason see the truth aright
Still woud you tread in virtues way
Remove the hindrance & you may
Banish Joy & banish love
Banish hope & banish fear
The mind has clouds we run astray
& reason's captive when they sway

On Sr Charles Porter The Chancellours Death

& tis too true alass! we find, he's gonn,
Virtue from earth a second time is flown,
She onely then with her two sisters flew,
But now since he, what ere were good withdrew;
Uncertain where to fix, in him they lost their seat,
& had But Heaven as a sure retreat.
He Held ye scales when Justice Hand did shake:
When He, youd think that wisdomes self did speak.
He was with Honour blest, with Honesty, & praise,
Ev'n Blest with all we could desire but dayes:
& those were much too few, for he is gon
(Not for himself but for ye world) too soon.
In him we found, & with him buried lies
What ever poets gave their deity's,
Joves Brow, Minervas learning, Hermes tongue
Apollo's wisdom, yeares, & his still seeming young;
The same sweet temper he to all did shew,
& as his face his mind no wrinkle knew.
He when with foes opprest was still ye same,
Pittying forgave, & smiling overcame.
This glorious sunn, like Heavens, was o're cast

By enymies, as that By clouds opprest,
That keepes his lookes compos'd, & this his breast.
Both do in glory sett, as both in glory reign,
But this for ever, that to rise again.
Perfections here as to their centre flowd,
He was tho great, yet farr from being proud.
Was gentle, liberall, & tho modest free,
Gold has allay, nay ev'ry thing but he.
Yet is he tak'n away snatcht hence by heaven
As if it seemd to envy what 't had given.
But when we've such a loss—
How can ye planetts shine ye cloudes not melt to rain
But ev'ry thing their wonted course retain.
Heav'n in our sorrow cannot have a share
We've lost a god on earth 't has got a saint a starr

Ye Wives Who Scold & Fishes Sell

Ye Wives who scold & fishes sell,
Or sing & sell your fruit,
I want a wondrous thing to tell,
Then (if you can) be mute.
From some of You one Homer came,
Who wrote a ballad first,
For He knew neither Parents name
Nor livd where he was nurst
His verse in length exceeds us all
So when a crowd he drew,
Like you he got him to a stall,
& spoke as long as you.
Some tatterd Mermaid gave him birth
Who crys her oyster wares
Or Else some ragged nymph of earth
Who sings her Mellow pears
If 'twas the nymph of fruit was prest,
Apollo was ye Lover:
With tunefull cry he filld her breast,
& got a singing Rover.
A Man, tho blind, yet usd to ply
Where 'ere he heard of Chear;
His dog it seems preserved an eye,
Its Master livd by ear.
Or if Apollo chancd to Love
The Mermaid near ye sea,
Whose shriller voice he taught to move
With buy my oysters pray.
Her shriller voice when raised to Ire
Woud thunder on ye crew,
So from ye Mother & ye Sire
Old Homers Iliad grew.

& then (as big with child she stood)
The place she sold her fishes
Might in his fancy form a floud
To rage in all th' Odysses.

The Soul in Sorrow

With kind compassion hear my cry
O Jesu, Lord of life, on high!
As when the Summer's seasons beat
With scorching flame and parching heat,
The trees are burnt, the flowers fade,
And thirsty gaps in earth are made,
My thoughts of comfort languish so,
And so my soul is broke by woe.
Then on thy servant's drooping head,
Thy dews of blessing sweetly shed;
Let those a quick refreshment give
And raise my mind, and bid me live.
My fears of danger while I breath,
My dread of endless hell beneath,
My sense of sorrow for my sin,
To springing comfort, change within,
Change all my sad complaints for ease,
To chearful notes of endless praise;
Nor let a tear mine eyes employ
But such as owe their birth to joy:
Joy transporting sweet and strong,
Fit to fill and raise my song,
Joy that shall resounded be
While days and nights succeed for me:
Be not as a Judge severe,
For so thy presence who may bear?
On all my words and actions look,
(I know they're written in thy book)
But then regard my mournful cry
And look with Mercy's gracious eye,
What needs my blood since thine will do
To pay the debt to justice due.
O tender mercy's art divine!
Thy sorrow proves the cure of mine,
Thy dropping wounds, thy woful smart,
Allay the bleedings of my heart:
Thy death, in death's extreme of pain,
Restores my soul to life again.
Guide me then for here I burn
To make my Saviour some return.
I'll rise, (if that will please him still
And sure I've heard him own it will)

I'll trace his steps and bear my cross
Despising ev'ry grief and loss;
Since he despising pain and shame,
First took up his, and did the same.

www.ingramcontent.com/pod-product-compliance
Lightning Source LLC
Chambersburg PA
CBHW060145050426
42448CB00010B/2310